Mathematics for

Practical Activities in Mathematics

Teacher's Book

M. R. Heylings M.A., M.Sc.

Schofield & Sims Limited Huddersfield

© 1989 Schofield & Sims Ltd.

All rights reserved.
No part of this publication may be reproduced,
stored in a retrieval system, or transmitted
in any form, or by any means, electronic,
mechanical, photocopying, recording or otherwise,
without the prior permission of Schofield & Sims Ltd.

0 7217 2433 7

First printed 1989

Books by the same author,
in the series **Graded examples in mathematics**:

Fractions and Decimals	0 7217 2323 3
Answer Book	0 7217 2324 1
Algebra	0 7217 2325 x
Answer Book	0 7217 2326 8
Area and Volume	0 7217 2327 6
Answer Book	0 7217 2328 4
General Arithmetic	0 7217 2329 2
Answer Book	0 7217 2330 6
Geometry and Trigonometry	0 7217 2331 4
Answer Book	0 7217 2332 2
Negative Numbers and Graphs	0 7217 2333 0
Answer Book	0 7217 2334 9
Matrices and Transformations	0 7217 2335 7
Answer Book	0 7217 2336 5
Sets, Probability and Statistics	0 7217 2337 3
Answer Book	0 7217 2338 1
Revision of Topics	0 7217 2339 x
Answer Book	0 7217 2340 3

Designed by Graphic Art Concepts, Leeds
Printed in England by Pindar Print Limited, Scarborough, North Yorkshire

Contents

		page
Activity	1 · The building site	4
	2 · Bees and honeycombs	4
	3 · Fencing a vegetable plot	6
	4 · Labels and tins	8
	5 · The farmer's sheep hurdles	11
	6 · Edging a carpet	12
	7 · Arches and arcs	13
	8 · Easter egg boxes	15
	9 · Thermos flasks and heat loss	18
	10 · Electricity pylons and triangles	20
	11 · Mr Jackson's fencing	21
	12 · Cubes and boxes	22
	13 · Drainage channels	26
	14 · Footbridges	31
	15 · Ice-cream cones	33
	16 · Fruit farm cartons	34
	17 · Making ice lollipops	38
	18 · Street lighting	40
	19 · Coils of string	43
	20 · Stepping along	44
	21 · Pins and mirrors	46
	22 · Making a pantograph	48
	23 · Crank and piston	49
	24 · Manoeuvring around corners	52
	25 · Wrapping a parcel	53
	26 · Free gifts with breakfast cereal	56
	27 · Radioactive decay	57
	28 · In a nuclear reactor	59
	29 · Queuing at the corner shop	60
	30 · Queuing at the supermarket	64

1 · The building site

This activity reinforces the concept of area by finding the area of the given shape using various methods; furthermore, in using an *irregular* shape, pupils do not come to regard the concept of area as applying only to regular shapes. Method **2** requires some introductory explanation of how an area of 1 cm² can be associated with each dot: reference to Method **1** would be appropriate. Further problem **B** requires no prior knowledge of the formula $A = \pi r^2$, and it should only appear as a consequence of the practical activity. A graph of A against r^2 could also be drawn and its equation found.

Area of the building site is 108 hectares.

Area of the map of mainland Italy is 98.2 cm², so the area of mainland Italy is 2500 × 98.2 = 245 500 km², which can be compared with 251 500 km² from reference books.

2 · Bees and honeycombs

This activity explores which regular polygons tessellate and, for those which do, how many are needed to cover a given area. A reason can then be suggested to explain why bees build their cells with hexagonal cross-sections; the method which pupils use helps to reinforce their concept of perimeter.

Introduction

Of the regular polygons, only the triangle, square and hexagon tessellate because, only for them, is the 360° of a full turn a multiple of their interior angles (i.e. 60°, 90° and 120° respectively).

More able pupils might appreciate an algebraic treatment. A tessellation requires 360° to be a multiple of the interior angle of $180° - \frac{360°}{n}$ of the regular n-sided polygon.

That is, $\dfrac{360}{180 - \frac{360}{n}} = \dfrac{2n}{n-2} = 2 + \dfrac{4}{n-2}$ must be an integer, which is only the case when $n = 3$, 4 or 6.

All the given regular polygons have areas of 25 cm² and have sides as follows:

7.6 cm triangle ; 5.0 cm square ; 3.6 cm pentagon
3.1 cm hexagon ; 2.6 cm heptagon ; 2.3 cm octagon.

The honeycomb

Results will depend on how pupils position their tessellations over the large square. Approximate results give 32 triangles (with a total length of shared perimeter of about 425 cm), 36 squares (with about 420 cm) and 33 hexagons (with about 373 cm). From which, it seems that triangular cells use *most* wax and hexagon cells *least* wax. The bees, to be as economical as possible, make **hexagonal** cells in their honeycomb.

If pupils repeated this procedure with smaller polygons, the difference would be more pronounced. Any such repetitions, as a shared task amongst interested pupils, could be done by accurate drawing and measuring. For abler pupils, the extensions provide an algebraic treatment.

Extensions

A The first line of 4 triangles needs 2 + 5 + 2 sides.
The second and subsequent lines need 5 + 2 sides.
So, the total number of sides in a network of
m layers is $2 + m(5 + 2)$.
Similar results can be found for lines of more than 4 triangles.
In general, for m layers of n triangles, the total
number of sides is $\frac{n}{2} + m\left(n + 1 + \frac{n}{2}\right)$.

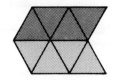

B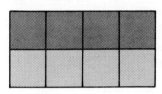

The first line of 4 squares needs 4 + 5 + 4 sides.
The second and subsequent lines need 5 + 4 sides.
So, the total number of sides in a network of
m layers is $4 + m(5 + 4)$.
In general, for m layers of n squares, the total number of sides is
$n + m(n + 1 + n) = 2mn + m + n$.

C The first line of 4 hexagons needs $(6 \times 4) - 3$ sides.
The second and subsequent lines need 7 sides fewer,
where $7 = 2 \times 4 - 1$.
So, the total number of sides in a network of
m layers is $m(6 \times 4 - 3) - (m - 1)(2 \times 4 - 1)$.
In general, for m layers of n hexagons, the total
number of sides is
$m[6n - (n - 1)] - (m - 1)(2n - 1) = 3mn + 2m + 2n - 1$.

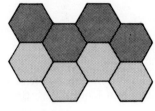

These formulae can be used to estimate the wax needed in the 30 cm square honeycomb when much smaller cells are used.
For example, with cells of area 1 cm², the square has sides of 1 cm, the triangle has sides of 1.52 cm and the hexagon has sides of 0.62 cm.

For a triangular tessellation
$0.76 \times n \simeq 30$ giving $n = 40$
$1.32 \times m \simeq 30$ giving $m = 22$
the total number of sides $= \frac{n}{2} + \left(n + 1 + \frac{n}{2}\right)m = 1362$
so, the total length of sides $= 1362 \times 1.52 = 2070$ cm

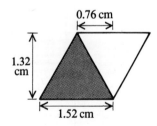

For a square tessellation
$1 \times n = 30$ giving $n = 30$
$1 \times m = 30$ giving $m = 30$
the total number of sides $= 2mn + m + n = 1860$
so, the total length of sides $= 1860 \times 1 = 1860$ cm

For a hexagonal tessellation
$0.93 \times n \simeq 30$ giving $n = 32$
$1.61 \times m \simeq 30$ giving $m = 19$
the total number of sides $= 3mn + 2m + 2n - 1 = 1925$
so, the total length of sides $= 1925 \times 0.62 = 1193$ cm

The total length of the sides is considerably smaller for the hexagonal tessellation, thus confirming the result found from the practical activity.

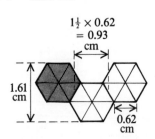

3 · Fencing a vegetable plot

This activity, by emphasising that shapes of the same area can have different perimeters, helps pupils to distinguish between the often confused concepts of *area* and *perimeter*.

The problem

Length of rectangle, cm	Width of rectangle, cm	Area of rectangle, cm^2	Perimeter of rectangle, cm
36	1	36	74
18	2	36	40
12	3	36	30
9	4	36	26
6	6	36	24
4	9	36	26
3	12	36	30
2	18	36	40
1	36	36	74

The smallest perimeter of 24 cm occurs when a square is formed. The minimum length of fence for Mr Smith is 24 metres.

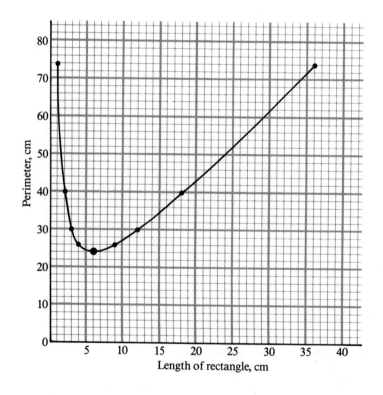

Further problems

A

Length of rectangle, cm	Width of rectangle, cm	Area of rectangle, cm²	Perimeter of rectangle, cm
24	1	24	50
12	2	24	28
8	3	24	22
6	4	24	20
4	6	24	20
3	8	24	22
2	12	24	28
1	24	24	50

The table indicates a minimum perimeter when the length and width lie between 4 and 6 cm. A calculator can now be used to explore more closely and, given a length, used to find the width and hence the perimeter.

For example

Length, cm	5.0	4.9	4.8
Width, cm	4.8	4.898	5.0
Perimeter, cm	19.6	19.596	19.6

The smallest perimeter occurs when a square of side 4.9 cm is formed. Note that $\sqrt{24} = 4.9$. The shortest fence for Mr Shaw is $4.9 \times 4 = 19.6$ metres.

Some pupils might appreciate an algebraic treatment for a rectangle of length x cm and width y cm, having an area of $xy = 24$ cm² and a perimeter of

$$2x + 2y = 2x + \frac{48}{x} \text{ cm}$$

which is the equation of the curve drawn by pupils. Evidence for a minimum value of perimeter is strong, though calculus would be needed to *prove* a minimum.

B

Length, cm	Width, cm	Area, cm²	Perimeter, cm
18	1	18	38
9	2	18	22
6	3	18	18
3	6	18	18
2	9	18	22
1	18	18	38

then using a calculator for lengths and widths between 3 cm and 6 cm

4	4.5	18	17
4.25	4.235	18	16.97
4.24	4.245	18	16.97

The minimum perimeter of 17.0 cm (to 1 decimal place) occurs when a square of side 4.24 cm is formed. Note that $\sqrt{18} = 4.24$.

The shortest fence of 17.0 miles will surround a square of side 4.24 miles.

4 · Labels and tins

This activity involves measuring the diameters and circumferences of various circular cross-sections, and so leads to the formula $C = \pi d$ which should *not* be given to pupils; it should arise from their own work. The extension sets a different problem of a spatial kind involving the 'best' way of arranging three 2-dimensional shapes.

The problem

Possible results are given in this table. It is unlikely that pupils' practical work will arrive at results as accurate as these.

Length of label, l cm	10	14	18	22	26	30	Average
Diameter of tin, d cm	3.2	4.5	5.7	7.0	8.3	9.5	
$\dfrac{l}{d}$	3.13	3.11	3.16	3.14	3.13	3.16	3.14

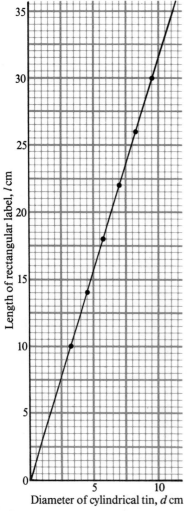

7 a A diameter of 8 cm needs a label 25.1 cm long.

b A diameter of 11 cm needs a label 34.5 cm long.

c A label 9 cm long is made for a tin of diameter 2.9 cm.

8

	Length of label, cm	Diameter of tin, cm
Tuna steak	21.0	6.7
Tomato puree	16.5	5.3
Baked beans	23.0	7.3

9 $\dfrac{l}{d} = 3.14$ giving $l = 3.14 \times d$

An extension

The work so far in this activity has not involved the height h of the tin. The height h and the diameter d are independent variables, i.e. the value of one does not affect the value of the other. A practical way of working towards a solution is to choose reasonable values of d and h which give arrangements which can be drawn full-size on A4 paper. A pupil's first ploy could then be to cut out the 3 pieces and try several arrangements. By drawing the enclosing rectangle and taking measurements with a ruler, areas can be found and various arrangements compared.

As d and h are independent variables, it is best not to alter both simultaneously; in the following analysis, d is fixed and h varies. Having found the best arrangement for the first choice of d and h, a pupil might begin to realise that only the value of (say) h need be altered. Some pupils might start with large values of h; thin slivers can then be cut away as h decreases (thus economising on paper) — other pupils might 'see' the problem more easily if h increases from initially small values.

Some pupils may find solutions only by cutting, arranging, drawing and measuring to compare arrangements. Able pupils may treat the problem algebraically once they have gained experience first by cutting and arranging.

In each of these arrangements, the area used in making the tin is

$$\pi dh + 2 \times \pi\left(\frac{d}{2}\right)^2 = \pi dh + \tfrac{1}{2}\pi d^2.$$

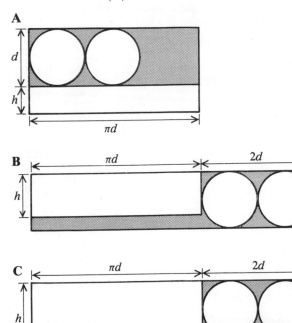

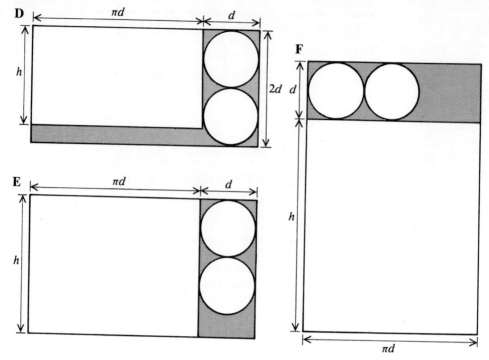

The total area of the enclosing rectangle in each arrangement is:

- **A** $\pi d (h + d)$
- **B** $d (\pi d + 2d)$
- **C** $h (\pi d + 2d)$
- **D** $2d (\pi d + d)$
- **E** $h (\pi d + d)$
- **F** $\pi d (h + d)$

Note that arrangements **A** and **F** are essentially the same.

Arrangement **B** becomes more economical than arrangement **A** when
$d (\pi d + 2d) < \pi d (h + d)$ giving $h > 0.64d$.

Similar considerations make **D** more economical than **C** when $h > 1.61d$
and **F** more economical than **E** when $h > \pi d$.

Summarising, the values can be placed on an h-line:

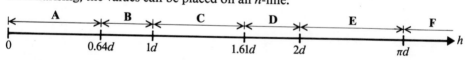

However, a slightly more economical arrangement is possible instead of **C**. It can be shown that **Z** is more economical than **D** when $h < 1.71d$.

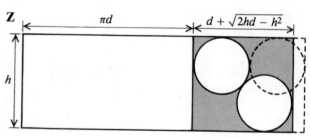

The h-line now becomes:

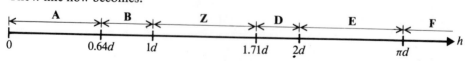

In reality, the rectangular pieces needed for the curved surface of the tins would probably be cut from one large sheet, with little waste as the rectangles will tessellate and the circular ends cut from a second sheet.

5 · The farmer's sheep hurdles

By emphasising that shapes of the same perimeter can have different areas, this activity helps pupils to distinguish between the concepts of *area* and *perimeter*.

Using a dotted grid to find area is suggested for its simplicity and speed of operation; other methods might be tried, perhaps as a cross-check, if pupils are confident with them.

The problem

Many possible areas may be enclosed in the loop; this table gives a few possibilities:

Shape	Estimate of area, cm^2
Rectangle 17 cm by 1 cm	17
Equilateral triangle	62
Rectangle 12 cm by 6 cm	72
Square	81
Regular hexagon	94
Circle	103

4 The greatest area occurs when the loop is a circle (of diameter 11.5 cm). Farmer Giles should arrange his hurdles in as near a circular shape as possible.

5 Mrs Auty should choose a circular cake tin.

Extensions

A The pupil should make a circular loop on dotted paper.
 The area of the circle is 32 cm^2.

B For a square, of edge x cm, perimeter = $4x$ = 36 cm so $x = 9$
 area of square = $9^2 = 81$ cm^2.
 For a rectangle of length 17 cm, width = $\frac{1}{2} \times 36 - 7 = 1$ cm
 area of rectangle = $17 \times 1 = 17$ cm^2.
 For a circle, circumference = $2\pi r$ so radius = $\frac{36}{2\pi} = 5.7$ cm
 area of circle = $\pi \times 5.7^2 = 103$ cm^2.

Further problems

The pupils' knowledge of the formulae is assumed in these problems.

a 'Largest' in this sense means 'with the fattest trunk', rather than 'tallest'.
 For a trunk with a circular cross-section of diameter d, $100 = \pi \times d$
 so largest diameter = $\frac{100}{\pi} = 31.8$ cm.

b   For a length of 10 metres, width = $\frac{1}{2}(26 - 2 \times 10) = 3$ metres.
Area of lawn = $10 \times 3 = 30$ m².
For a circular lawn, $26 = 2\pi \times r$ so radius $r = \frac{26}{2\pi} = 4.1$ metres.
Diameter of circular lawn = 8.2 metres.
Area of circular lawn = $\pi \times 4.1^2 = 52.8$ m².

6 · Edging a carpet

This activity is a development of the previous one *'The Farmer's Sheep Hurdles'*, which dealt with a variety of different shapes. In this activity, only rectangles having the same perimeters are considered.

The problem

Possible results are given in this table.

Length of rectangle, cm	Width of rectangle, cm	Its perimeter, cm	Its area, cm²
9	1	20	9
8	2	20	16
7	3	20	21
6	4	20	24
5	5	20	25
4	6	20	24
3	7	20	21
2	8	20	16
1	9	20	9

The pattern of results suggests that the largest area occurs with a square.
The maximum area of carpet which Mrs Preston can edge is 25 m² when the carpet is a square 5 m by 5 m.

To explore further, a calculator can be used for non-integer values. For example, the following results can be calculated.

Length l, cm	Width w, cm	Area A, cm²
4.9	5.1	24.99
4.99	5.01	24.9999
5	5	25
5.01	4.99	24.9999

These results provide further evidence of a maximum value of area.

Some pupils might appreciate an algebraic treatment for a rectangle of length l and width w. The perimeter of $2l + 2w = 20$ gives $w = 10 - l$, so the equation of the curve is given by area $A = l(10 - l)$.

(The use of calculus would *prove* that a maximum value of area exists.)

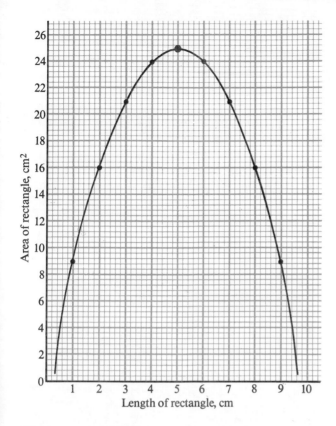

Extensions

A The largest area of lawn is 36 m² when it has the shape of a square of edge 6 metres.

B The largest area of cross-section is 1.5 × 1.5 = 2.25 m² when the duct has a square cross-section of edge 6 ÷ 4 = 1.5 metres.

7 · Arches and arcs

This 2-dimensional spatial activity requiring accurate drawing and measuring, invites pupils to explore the construction of arches from two circular arcs.

The problem

Possible results for span AB of 6 cm are given in this table.

Radius of arc, r cm	3	4	6	8	10	12	14
Height of arch, h cm	3.0	3.9	5.2	6.2	7.1	7.9	8.7

The smallest possible radius is $\frac{1}{2} \times AB$ in which case the centres of the two arcs coincide at the midpoint of AB and the arch has a semicircular shape.

A 6 metre span and an arch 7 metres high require circular arcs of radius 9.7 metres.

An extension

Different spans give the following results:

Radius of arc, r cm		4	5	6	7	8	10	12	14
Height of arch, for h cm	AB = 8 cm	4.0	4.9	5.7	6.3	6.9	8.0	8.9	9.8
	AB = 10 cm	—	5.0	5.9	6.7	7.4	8.7	9.7	10.7
	AB = 12 cm	—	—	6.0	6.9	7.7	9.2	10.4	11.5
	AB = 14 cm	—	—	—	7.0	7.9	9.5	10.9	12.1

An arch 8 metres high can be built with a span AB and a radius of 6 m and 12.2 m
   or 8 m and 10.0 m
   or 10 m and 8.9 m
   or 12 m and 8.3 m
   or 14 m and 8.1 m respectively.

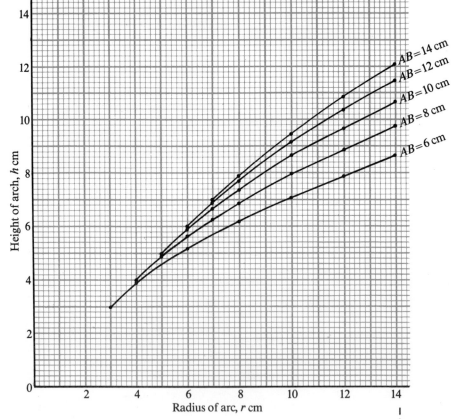

More able pupils might confirm their empirical results as follows.
Taking the span AB as x and using Pythagoras' theorem,
$$h^2 + \left(r - \frac{x}{2}\right)^2 = r^2$$
giving $h = \sqrt{rx - \frac{x^2}{4}}$.

Substituting values for the span, x and the radius, r gives the height, h of the arch.

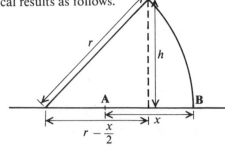

A further problem

There are many possible solutions to this problem.

The lowest arch (which also has the greatest span) is semicircular. This solution can be found by calculation. Other possibilities will be higher but narrower, and are easiest found by scale drawing.

The semicircular arch has a radius of 4.3 metres and a span of 8.6 metres.

Another possibility has a radius of 6 metres and a span of 6 metres.

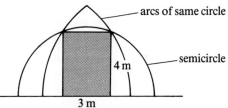

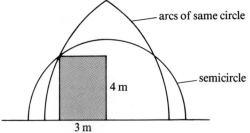

If, however, the lorry has to keep entirely to the left-hand side of the road, the semicircular arch has a radius of 5 metres and a span of 10 metres.

Another possibility has a radius of 7 metres and a span of 8.6 metres.

8 · Easter egg boxes

This 3-dimensional activity requires a systematic approach to finding all possible boxes and then helps to develop the pupils' concepts of surface area and edge length.

1 Two designs are possible for 3 eggs.

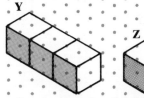

Eight designs are possible for 4 eggs.

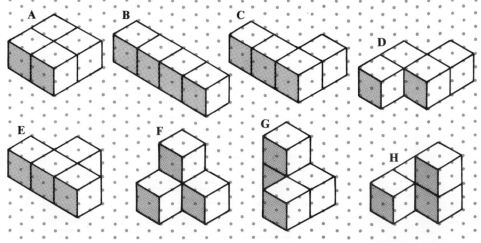

4-cube box	Surface area, sq. units	Edge length, units	Cost, pence
A	16	20	52
B	18	24	60
C	18	26	62
D	18	28	64
E	18	28	64
F	18	30	66
G	18	28	64
H	18	28	64

Box **A** is not only the cheapest to make, but is also a conventional design which is easy to make.

Extensions

A This is the Soma Cube puzzle. The Jumbo-size cube contains $6 \times 4 + 3 = 27$ eggs; thus, it is a $3 \times 3 \times 3$ cube. The pieces to use are **Z, C, D, E, F, G** and **H**, as labelled on the previous page.

B None of the nets are unique. One each of the many possibilities is drawn here.

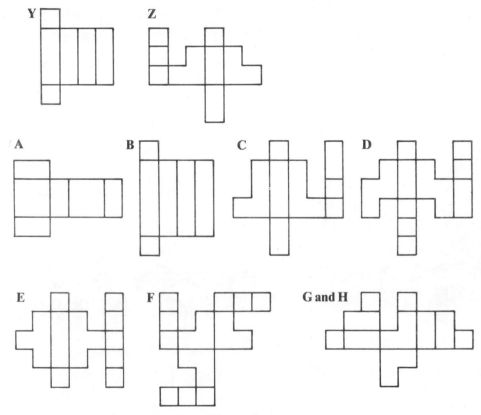

Note: the boxes **G** and **H** are the mirror images of each other; so, their nets are the same. However, when using the nets to make the boxes, the folds will be in the opposite direction.

Further problems

The solids **A** to **H** give all the possible shapes, but different orientations are possible. Pupils might decide that 'overhanging' rooms are not allowed; for example

Except for these, other possibilities are drawn below.

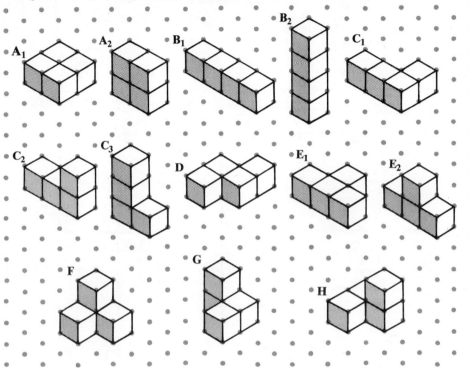

Apartment	Cost of building, £	Cost of insulation, £	Total cost, £
A_1	12 000	6 000	18 000
A_2	10 000	7 000	17 000
B_1	12 000	7 000	19 000
B_2	12 000	8 500	20 500
C_1	12 000	7 000	19 000
C_2	11 000	7 500	18 500
C_3	11 000	8 000	19 000
D	12 000	7 000	19 000
E_1	12 000	7 000	19 000
E_2	11 000	7 500	18 500
F	11 000	7 500	18 500
G	11 000	7 500	18 500
H	11 000	7 500	18 500

A_2 is the likeliest choice for the builder; it is not only the cheapest design but is also traditional and so likely attractive to buyers.

9 · Thermos flasks and heat loss

This spatial activity in 3-dimensions involves the concepts of volume and surface area. Their ratio is introduced as 'surface area per unit of volume' and the notion of *compactness* of a solid is used to help decide which shape is *'best'*.

The problem

The results are given in this table.

Solid	Volume, cubic units	Surface area, square units	Ratio $\frac{\text{surface area}}{\text{volume}}$
	1	6	6
	2	10	5
	3	14	$4\frac{2}{3} \simeq 4.7$
*	4	16	4
	4	18	$4\frac{1}{2} = 4.5$
*	5	20	4
and others	5	22	$4\frac{2}{5} = 4.4$

The single cube has the highest ratio, i.e. it has more surface area for its volume than any of the other solids; so, the single cube will lose its heat the quickest.

The most *compact* solids, indicated by *, made from 4 or 5 cubes have the smallest ratio, so they will lose their heat the slowest.

The following table gives some of the most compact arrangements with larger numbers of cubes.

Solid	Volume, cubic units	Surface area, square units	Ratio $\dfrac{\text{surface area}}{\text{volume}}$
	6	22	$3\frac{2}{3} \simeq 3.7$
	7	24	$3\frac{3}{7} \simeq 3.4$
	8	24	3
	9	30	$3\frac{1}{3} \simeq 3.3$
	9	28	$3\frac{1}{9} \simeq 3.1$
	12	36	3
	12	32	$2\frac{2}{3} \simeq 2.7$
	27	54	2

In general, for compact solids, the greater the volume, the smaller is the ratio; i.e. larger solids tend to have a smaller surface area relative to their volume.

For a thermos flask to lose as little heat as possible, it needs to be as 'compact' as possible. Such a design using 18 cubes would be 2 × 3 × 3, viz:

The *most* compact shape would be a sphere.

Extensions

A Young needing care to be kept warm after birth:
   chicks, puppies, kittens, mice, hedgehogs, human babies.

Young needing less special treatment:
   deer, calves, foals, sheep, goats, elephants, whales.

The smaller creatures need to be kept warm as their ratio of surface area to volume is higher, so they lose their body heat more quickly than larger babies. For the same reason, a human baby needs more protective clothing than an adult.

B The fins dissipate the heat from inside the refrigerator to the surrounding air. By making the fins large and flat (rather than small and round), their surface area is increased and so they lose their heat more quickly.

C Warm-blooded animals need to lose heat at times so as to control their temperature. Humans sweat through their skins; dogs pant and lose heat through their tongues and mouths. It is thought by some that the stegosaurus lost heat through its fins, which increased its surface area, rather like the fins on the back of the refrigerator.

10 · Electricity pylons and triangles

This activity involves accurate drawing and measuring and provides a practical example of a function in which the length of the base of an isosceles triangle is dependent on the size of the opposite angle.

The problem

Possible results are given in this table.

Angle, $a°$	0	10	30	60	90	120	150	180
Distance, d cm	0	1.7	5.2	10.0	14.1	17.3	19.3	20.0

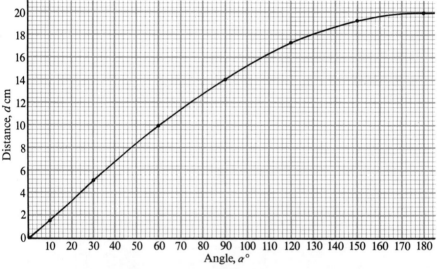

Pupils will need dividers 10 cm long to check their graphical answers by measurement. If none are available, they could be provided with strips of card 10 cm long, hinged at one end with a paper fastener.

3 a When $a = 90°$, $d = 14.1$ cm.

  b A scale factor of 100 converts centimetres to metres. When $d = 2$ cm, angle $a = 11.5°$.

  c A scale factor of 500 is involved. Feet 10 metres apart scale down to a distance apart of 2 cm. Angle $a = 11.5°$ as in part **b**.

  d A scale factor of 25 is involved. A distance of 1 metre scales down to 4 cm. So, angle $a = 23°$.

  e A scale factor of $1\frac{1}{2}$ is involved. When $a = 65°$, $d = 10.7$ cm, so radius of circle is $1.5 \times 10.7 = 16.1$ cm.

For pupils with some knowledge of trigonometry, these results could be predicted from $d = 2 \times 10 \sin \frac{a}{2}$.

11 · Mr Jackson's fencing

Given the length of the equal sides of an isosceles triangle, this activity discovers how the angle between these sides affects the area of the triangle.

The problem

When $\alpha = 0°$ or $180°$, the area enclosed by the fencing and wall is zero. As other values of α give non-zero values for the area, we suspect that a maximum value of the area exists between $\alpha = 0°$ and $\alpha = 180°$.

Angle, $\alpha°$	0	10	30	60	90	120	150	180
Area of triangle, cm²	0	8.7	25.0	43.3	50.0	43.3	25.0	0

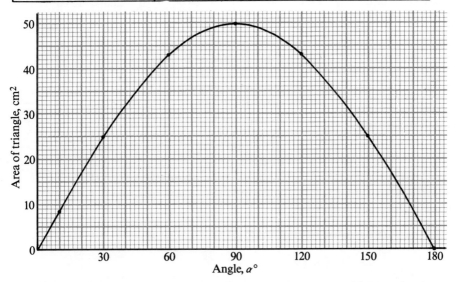

The graph shows that, for the maximum enclosed area, the angle between the two fences should be 90°. In this position, the area is 50 square metres and the triangle is right-angled and isosceles.

Pupils familiar with trigonometry could check their results as follows:

Area of triangle $= \frac{1}{2} AB \times h$

$= xh$

$= 10 \sin \frac{\alpha}{2} \times 10 \cos \frac{\alpha}{2}$

$= 100 \sin \frac{\alpha}{2} \cos \frac{\alpha}{2} = 50 \sin \alpha$

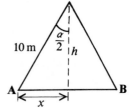

Angle, $\alpha°$	Area of triangle, cm²
89	49.992385
89.5	49.998096
89.9	49.999924
90	50
90.1	49.999924
90.5	49.998096

The use of a calculator can now further explore the position of the maximum. For example, these results can be obtained which add further evidence to the maximum occuring when angle $\alpha = 90°$.
(Calculus could *prove* that the maximum occurs when $\alpha = 90°$.)

A further problem

Maximum storage requires maximum area of cross-section which occurs when the two rectangular sheets make an angle of 90° with each other.
In this position,
  area of cross-section = $\frac{1}{2} \times 5 \times 5 = 12\frac{1}{2}$ m²
  so, greatest volume = $12\frac{1}{2} \times 12 = 150$ m³

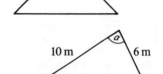

Extensions

A Scale drawing of triangles as before (though *not* isosceles triangles in this case) gives these results:

Angle, $a°$	0	10	30	60	90	120	150	180
Area of triangle, m²	0	5.2	15.0	26.0	30.0	26.0	15.0	0

A graph can be drawn. The maximum area occurs (as before) when $a = 90°$ and its value is 30 m².

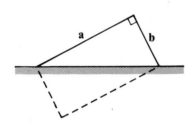

Other lengths of fencing will also produce maximum areas when $a = 90°$. Pupils should 'see' the generalised value of the area from the numerical pattern of their answers before being asked to prove it — either by considering half a rectangle or by re-orientating the triangle to have a base b and a height a.

Pupils familiar with trigonometry could check their results as follows:
  Area of triangle = $\frac{1}{2}b \times h$
    = $\frac{1}{2}b \times a \sin a$
    = $\frac{1}{2} ab \sin a$

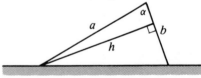

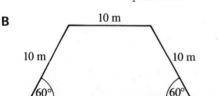

B Maximum area = 129.9 m²

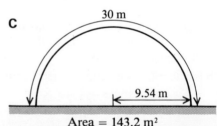

C Area = 143.2 m²

12 · Cubes and boxes

This activity encourages both 2- and 3-dimensional imagination and dexterity. Pupils could be prompted to develop a systematic approach to finding *all* the possible nets.

The problem

1,2 There are 12 pentominoes; 8 of them are possible nets of an open box, 4 of them are not.

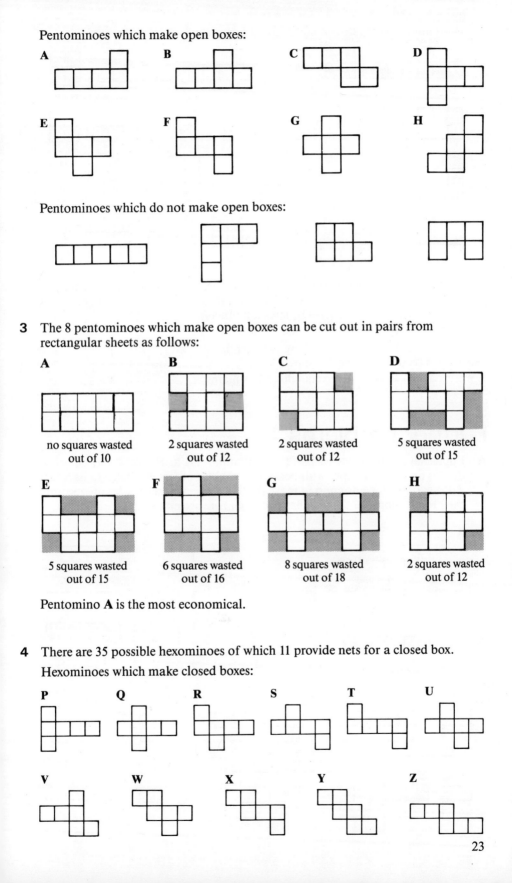

Hexominoes which do not make closed boxes:

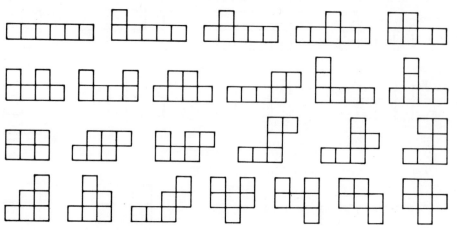

Note: these hexominoes have been drawn in an order which classifies them as having a 'horizontal' spine of 6 squares (1 diagram), 5 squares (3 diagrams), 4 squares (7 diagrams), 3 squares (all others).

The most economical way of making two identical nets from a rectangular sheet is shown here. It wastes only 4 squares in a rectangle of 16 squares.

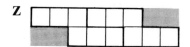

Further problems

A Pupils have to tessellate each of the pentominoes **A** to **H**. Some may be able to do this on squared paper with pencil and rubber; others may need to have (say) a dozen of each pentomino to make the tessellation physically before recording their result. Some of the tessellations given here are not unique.

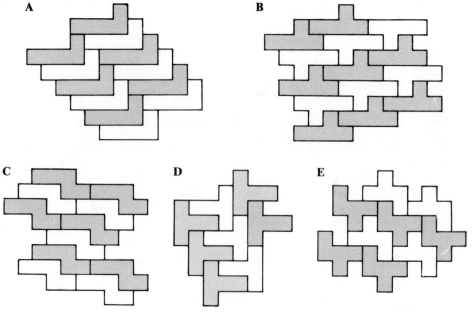

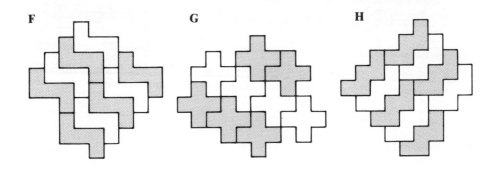

The above diagrams show that all the pentominoes will tessellate. Any wastage of the large rectangular sheets will thus occur only at its edges.

The following diagrams show that all eleven hexominoes **P** to **Z** also tessellate.

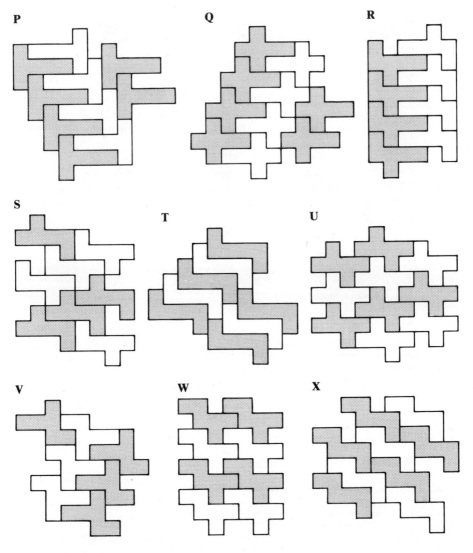

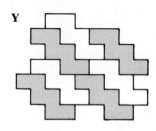
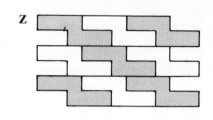

B The manufacturer will have to leave gaps in the tessellations, as shown here for **G** and **Q**.

Tabs are shown in grey; black areas are waste.

For **G**, the pentominoes have been separated by one half unit 'vertically'.

For **Q**, the hexominoes have been separated by one unit 'vertically' and half a unit 'horizontally'.

G   **Q**

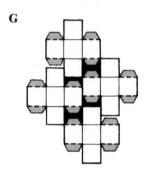
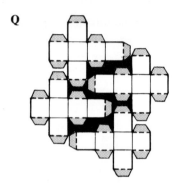

Consider nets for *closed* boxes. Pentominoes all have perimeters 12 units long and thus need 6 tabs. Hexominoes all have perimeters 14 units long and thus need 7 tabs. One rule for positioning tabs around the perimeter is simply 'put one, miss one, put one, miss one . . . '; i.e. every alternate edge.

13 · Drainage channels

Although ostensibly a 3-D spatial problem, this activity deals in 2-dimensions with rectangular areas of cross-section. It differs from Activity **6**, *'Edging a carpet'*, where the whole perimeter of the rectangle was constant; here, only 3 of the 4 sides have a constant total length. As in Activity **11**, as sides giving zero height and zero width both give zero area, intuitively a maximum area of cross-section can be expected for an intermediate value.

The problem

3 Possible results are given in this table:

Width of central strip, cm	0	1	2	3	4	5	6	7	8	9	10
Width of side strips, cm	5	$4\frac{1}{2}$	4	$3\frac{1}{2}$	3	$2\frac{1}{2}$	2	$1\frac{1}{2}$	1	$\frac{1}{2}$	0
Area of cross-section, cm^2	0	$4\frac{1}{2}$	8	$10\frac{1}{2}$	12	$12\frac{1}{2}$	12	$10\frac{1}{2}$	8	$4\frac{1}{2}$	0

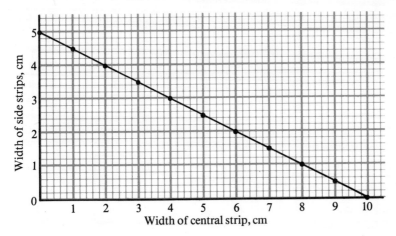

4 The graph shows that the maximum area of $12\frac{1}{2}$ cm² occurs when the channel is 5 cm wide and $2\frac{1}{2}$ cm high.

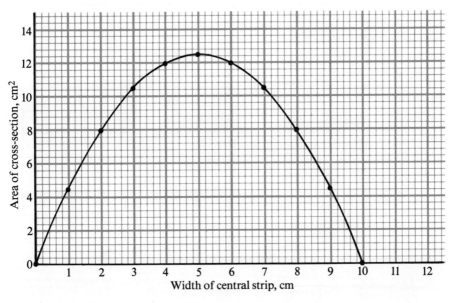

When the width of the central strip is known, these two graphs allow the width of the side strips and the cross-sectional area to be found without any further calculation.

A calculator can help to provide further evidence of the maximum by considering non-integer values for the widths of the strips. (Calculus could provide a *proof* of the maximum.) For example:

Width of central strip, cm	Width of side strips, cm	Area of cross-section, cm²
4.8	2.6	12.48
4.9	2.55	12.495
4.98	2.51	12.4998
5	2.5	12.5
5.02	2.49	12.4998
5.1	2.45	12.495

5 Results for paper strips of different widths are as follows:

Overall strip width of 6 cm:

Width of central strip, cm	0	1	2	3	4	5	6
Width of side strips, cm	3	$2\frac{1}{2}$	2	$1\frac{1}{2}$	1	$\frac{1}{2}$	0
Area of cross-section, cm²	0	$2\frac{1}{2}$	4	$4\frac{1}{2}$	4	$2\frac{1}{2}$	0

Overall strip width of 8 cm:

Width of central strip, cm	0	2	4	6	8
Width of side strips, cm	4	3	2	1	0
Area of cross-section, cm²	0	6	8	6	0

Overall strip width of 12 cm:

Width of central strip, cm	0	2	4	6	8	10	12
Width of side strips, cm	6	5	4	3	2	1	0
Area of cross-section, cm²	0	10	16	18	16	10	0

Overall strip width of 14 cm:

Width of central strip, cm	2	4	6	7	8	10	12
Width of side strips, cm	6	5	4	$3\frac{1}{2}$	3	2	1
Area of cross-section, cm²	12	20	24	$24\frac{1}{2}$	24	20	12

Overall strip width of 16 cm:

Width of central strip, cm	2	4	6	8	10	12	14
Width of side strips, cm	7	6	5	4	3	2	1
Area of cross-section, cm²	14	24	30	32	30	24	14

Two families of graphs can now be drawn.

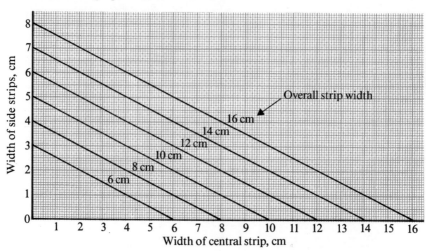

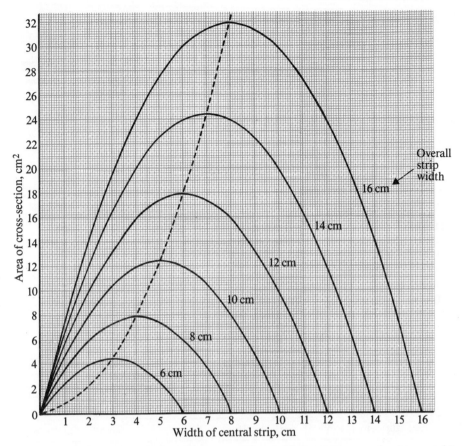

6 Conditions for maximum areas of cross-section can be brought together in one table.

Overall width of strip of paper, cm	6	8	10	12	14	16
Maximum area of cross-section, cm^2	$4\frac{1}{2}$	8	$12\frac{1}{2}$	18	$24\frac{1}{2}$	32
Width of central strip, cm	3	4	5	6	7	8
Width of side strips, cm	$1\frac{1}{2}$	2	$2\frac{1}{2}$	3	$3\frac{1}{2}$	4

Number patterns in this table include:
(i) width of central strip is half of the overall width of the paper
(ii) width of side strips is half of the width of the central strip or a quarter of the overall width of the paper
(iii) area of cross-section is the product of the widths of the central and side strips.

7 For the greatest area of cross-section, the central strip should be $\frac{1}{2} \times 2.4 = 1.2$ metres wide and the two side strips should be $\frac{1}{4} \times 1.2 = 0.6$ metres wide. The greatest area of cross-section is $1.2 \times 0.6 = 0.72$ m^2.

Extensions

A

Overall width of strip of paper, cm	20	24	28	30	60	100
Maximum area of cross-section, cm^2	50	72	98	$112\frac{1}{2}$	450	1250
Width of central strip, cm	10	12	14	15	30	50
Width of side strips, cm	5	6	7	$7\frac{1}{2}$	15	25

B If overall width of strip of paper $= x$ cm, then for the maximum area

of cross-section, width of central strip $= \dfrac{x}{2}$

width of each side strip $= \dfrac{x}{4}$

so, maximum area of cross-section $= \dfrac{x}{2} \times \dfrac{x}{4} = \dfrac{x^2}{8}$.

By substituting known values, this result can be checked.

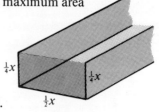

A further problem

As in Activity 11, there is an expectation of a maximum area of cross-section between the values $a = 0°$ and $a = 180°$, both of which give zero area of cross-section. However, with equal strip widths, there is also a physical limitation of $a < 120°$.

Pupils will need to cut out one channel to see the effect of altering the value of angle a. Scale drawings of the cross-section will give those values of length d and height h required to calculate the area of cross-section. For ease of computation, pupils will need prior knowledge of the formula for the area of a trapezium.

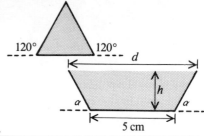

Results are as follows:

Angle, $a°$	0	20	40	60	80	100	120
Height, h cm	0	1.7	3.2	4.3	4.9	4.9	4.3
Length, d cm	15	14.4	12.7	10.0	6.7	3.3	0
Area of trapezium, cm²	0	16.6	28.4	32.5	28.8	20.3	10.8

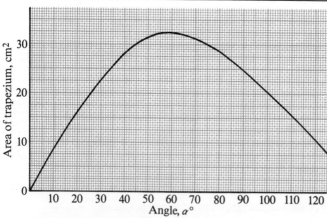

The graph shows that the maximum area of cross-section of 32.5 cm² occurs when angle $a = 60°$.

Pupils familiar with trigonometry may be able to show that $h = 5 \sin a$

$d = 5 + 2 \times 5 \cos a$

hence, area of cross-section $= \tfrac{1}{2}h(d + 5)$

$= 25 \sin a(1 + \cos a).$

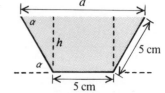

This formula could then be used to check the results obtained by scale drawing. Also, a stronger case can now be made for the maximum area of cross-section occurring when $a = 60°$.

Using a calculator or a short computer program,
  $\alpha = 59°$ gives area = 32.466027 cm²
  $\alpha = 59.9°$ gives area = 32.475854 cm²
  $\alpha = 60°$ gives area = 32.475953 cm²
  $\alpha = 60.1°$ gives area = 32.475854 cm²
  $\alpha = 61°$ gives area = 32.466094 cm².
The evidence for a maximum when $\alpha = 60°$ is now very strong. Calculus would be able to provide conclusive *proof*.

14 · Footbridges

The range of equipment required for this activity makes it akin to a science experiment. However, apart from the notion of force, pupils need no other background in science. In constructing and using several graphs, this activity develops a facility to interpret graphs and make predictions.

The problem

It might be pointed out to pupils that supporting a bridge from underneath as in the sketch is essentially the same as supporting it from above by suspension; both methods of support provide vertical forces; one by reaction with the buttress, the other by tension in the spring balance.

1,2 Possible results when a 2 kg mass is used, are:

Reading S, grams	1900	1660	1200	1000	660	400
Reading T, grams	260	500	960	1160	1500	1760

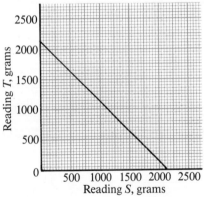

3 The greatest value of S occurs when the weight is hanging directly underneath S. For the above results, the maximum value of S would be 2080 grams and T would then be 80 grams.
Similarly, the greatest value of T occurs when the weight is hanging directly underneath T.

4 S and T have the same value (of 1080 grams) when the weight hangs from the centre of the rule.

5 If the metre rule is suspended 5 cm from each end, and a weight of 2 kg is used, then results similar to these will be obtained.

Distance, x cm	0	20	40	45	75	90
Reading S, grams	2080	1635	1190	1080	415	80

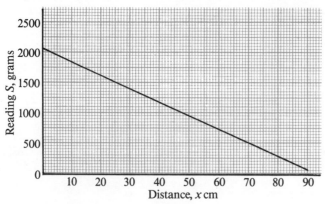

6 For a given value of x, the value of S can be found from one graph and then this value used to find the corresponding value of T from the other graph.
Possible results are:

Distance, x cm	0	20	40	45	75	90
Reading T, grams	80	525	970	1080	1745	2080

An extension

A wooden metre rule has a mass of about 150 grams.
The total mass hanging from the spring balance is the masses of the hanging object and the metre rule.
Possible results are:

Reading S, grams	1900	1660	1200	1000	660	400
Reading T, grams	260	500	960	1160	1500	1760
$S + T$	2160	2160	2160	2160	2160	2160

The value of $S + T$ is constant, regardless of where the hanging object is positioned. This value is the *total* mass hanging from the spring balances. In these results, with a hanging mass of 2 kg, it can be concluded that the metre rule has a mass of 160 grams. (Note that this result is found *without* direct measurement; as a check, the metre rule can now be weighed by itself.)

A further problem

Pupils need to appreciate that the *total* force at end S is found by simply *adding* the forces for the boy and girl separately.
For example, when the boy is 10 units from S, the girl is 40 units from S, so the graph of S against x can be used twice for $x = 10$ and $x = 40$ and the readings added.
Possible approximate results from the graph are:

Distance of boy from S, cm Distance of girl from S, cm	0 50	20 30	40 10	50 0
Force at S due to boy, kg Force at S due to girl, kg	2080 950	1650 1400	1200 1850	950 2080
Total force at S, kg	3030	3050	3050	3030

These results are approximate as no allowance has been made for the 5 cm overhang at the ends of the metre rule and as the addition of the forces for boy and girl includes the weight of the bridge twice. Even so, there is little variation in the total force at S.

When the boy walks twice as fast as the girl, approximate results from the graph are:

Distance of boy from S, cm	0	20	40	80	100
Distance of girl from S, cm	50	40	30	10	0
Force at S due to boy, kg	2080	1650	1200	300	0
Force at S due to girl, kg	950	1200	1400	1850	2080
Total force at S, kg	3030	2850	2600	2150	2080

It can be seen that the force at S is greatest when the boy and girl are in their initial positions.

15 · Ice-cream cones

In the simple construction of a cone from a sector of a circle, this activity provides a ready context for the idea of a function in which one variable (the height of the cone) depends on another variable (the radius of the circle).

The problem

2 Possible methods for measuring the height of the cone include:
   (i) using a sharp pencil and estimating where it protrudes from the base of the cone
   (ii) inserting a thin rod through the apex when the cone is standing on a flat surface.

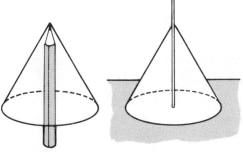

3 Possible results are given in this table. It is unlikely that pupils will arrive at results as accurate as these from practical work.

Radius of circle, cm	5	6	7	8	9	10	12	14	16
Vertical height of cone, cm	4.7	5.6	6.6	7.5	8.5	9.4	11.3	13.2	15.0

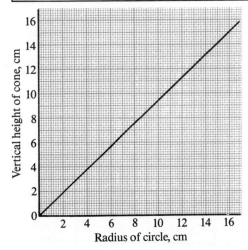

5   A cornet 7 cm high can be made from a circle of radius 7.4 cm.
6   A giant size cornet 10 cm high needs a circle of radius 10.6 cm.
7   Angels 5 cm high need a circle of radius 5.3 cm.

Extensions

The third row of the table gives values of $\frac{h}{r} = 0.94$.
The equation required is thus $h = 0.94r$.
Note that the gradient of the straight line graph is 0.94.

a   The height of the icing-bag is $0.94 \times 25 = 23.5$ cm.
b   The height of the witch's hat is $0.94 \times 30 = 28.2$ cm.
c   For a height of 25 cm, a radius of 26.6 cm will be needed.

These answers have been found empirically using the data obtained from the practical work. All the results can be checked theoretically by pupils who have some familiarity with the mensuration of circles and cones and with Pythagoras' theorem.

The arc of the circle becomes the circumference
of the base of the cone.

$\frac{1}{3} \times 2\pi r = 2\pi R$

So $R = \frac{1}{3}r$.

The radius of the circle becomes the
slant height of the cone.

Pythagoras' theorem gives $r^2 = h^2 + R^2$

hence $h = \sqrt{\frac{8}{9}} \times r = 0.94 \times r$.

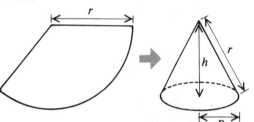

16 · Fruit farm cartons

This is a further problem involving the construction of a 3-dimensional container from its 2-dimensional net. Another context is given for the notion of a function. As in Activity **11**, the maximum value is intuitively expected as corners cut away with 0 cm and 9 cm sides produce no volume.

The problem

The drawing and cutting out of the net is made easier if pupils use paper ruled with a square grid. After pupils have constructed several boxes, economies can be made in the paper used by cutting away larger and larger corners from the same square.
Possible results are given in this table.

Side of corner square cut away, cm	Dimensions of box			Volume of box, cm³
	Length, cm	Width, cm	Height, cm	
1	16	16	1	256
2	14	14	2	392
3	12	12	3	432
4	10	10	4	400
5	8	8	5	320
6	6	6	6	216
7	4	4	7	112
8	2	2	8	32
9	0	0	9	0

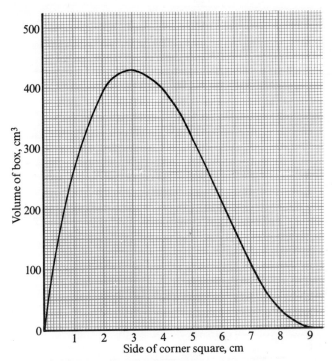

6 For a box with a volume of 300 cm^3, the graph shows that corner squares of side 1.25 cm or 5.2 cm should be cut away.

7 The graph shows that a maximum volume of 432 cm^3 occurs when the corner squares have sides of 3 cm. To explore whether this is an accurate result, a calculator can be used for non-integer lengths, for example:

a corner square of side 2.9 cm gives a volume of box of 431.636 cm^3
of side 2.95 cm gives a volume of box of 431.9095 cm^3
of side 3 cm gives a volume of box of 432 cm^3
of side 3.01 cm gives a volume of box of 431.9964 cm^3.

These figures provide stronger evidence for (but not *proof* of) a maximum of 432 cm^3.

Extensions

A A repeat of the above analysis with squares of different sizes gives the following summary of results which, when graphed, gives a family of curves.

Table of volumes of boxes, cm³

Side of original square, cm	Side of corner square cut away, cm											
	1	2	3	4	5	6	7	8	9	10	11	12
12	100	128	108	64	20	0	—	—	—	—	—	—
15	169	242	243	196	125	54	7	—	—	—	—	—
18	256	392	432	400	320	216	112	32	0	—	—	—
21	361	578	675	676	605	486	343	200	81	10	—	—
24	484	800	972	1024	980	864	700	512	324	160	44	0

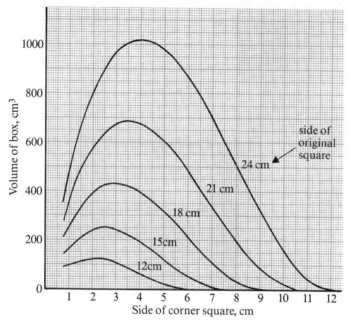

Investigations with the calculator will confirm the positions of the maximums and lead to these results:

Side of original square, cm	12	15	18	21	24
Maximum volume, cm³	128	250	432	686	1024
Side of corner square cut away, cm	2	2.4	3	3.5	4

The pattern of these results suggests that the maximum volume of the box occurs when the corner square cut away has a side one sixth the length of that of the original square.

A square of side 30 cm would thus require corner squares of side 5 cm to be cut away, giving a maximum volume of $25 \times 25 \times 5 = 3125$ cm³.

Some pupils might be able to find an algebraic expression for the volume of the box. If the original square has L cm and the corner square side x cm, then the volume of the box is
$V = x(L - 2x)^2$.

This expression could be used to generate results using a short computer program. For example,

```
10  PRINT "INPUT L AND X"
20  INPUT L, X
30  PRINT "DIMENSIONS OF BOX ARE"
40  PRINT X, L - 2 * X, L - 2 * X
50  PRINT "VOLUME OF BOX IS"
60  PRINT X * (L - 2 * X) ↑ 2
70  END
```

Calculus would *prove* that the maximum volume occurs when $x = \frac{1}{6}L$ and also that its value is $\frac{2}{27}L^3$. However, this expression can be estimated by numerical methods, as follows from the earlier result.

L	12	15	18	21	24
L^2	144	225	324	441	576
L^3	1728	3375	5832	9261	13824
Maximum volume, V	128	250	432	686	1024

Graphs of the maximum volume against increasing powers of length L until a straight line graph is obtained, give these results.

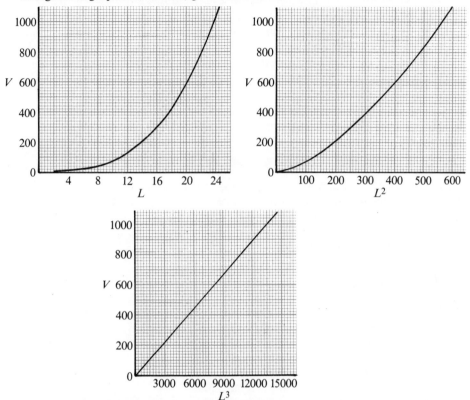

The graph of V against L^3 is linear. Its gradient is $1024/13824 = 0.074$, hence $V = 0.074 \times L^3$ which is a close approximation to the exact value of $\frac{2}{27}L^3$.

Suitable software would allow this curve-fitting exercise to be done on a computer.

B Drawing and cutting out the net from a rectangle 20 cm by 15 cm gives these results, from which a graph can be drawn.

Side of corner square cut away, cm	Dimensions of box			Volume of box, cm³
	Length, cm	Width, cm	Height, cm	
1	18	13	1	234
2	16	11	2	352
3	14	9	3	378
4	12	7	4	336
5	10	5	5	250
6	8	3	6	144
7	6	1	7	42

The graph indicates a maximum volume of approximately 379 cm³. Systematic trial-and-error using a calculator gives:

Side cut away, cm	Volume of box, cm³
2.8	379.008
2.85	379.0215
2.9	378.856

These figures provide stronger evidence of a maximum volume slightly in excess of 379 cm³ when corner squares of a side approximately 2.85 cm are cut away.

Calculus would *prove* that a maximum volume of 379.04 cm³ occurs when a side slightly less than 2.83 cm is used.

A computer programme similar to that in Extension **A** could be used to generate results.

17 · Making ice lollipops

This problem is allied to that in Activity **15**, except that here, the radius of the sector is fixed and the angle determines the volume of the cone.

The teacher is left to decide how long a time lapse is best left for a particular pupil between Activities **15** and **17**; i.e., whether clarity or confusion, interest or tedium, would ensue if they were attempted shortly after each other.

The problem

In discussion with pupils, either as part of an initial exploration of the problem or at some appropriate later time, it could be shown that as $\theta \to 0°$ or $360°$, the volume of the cone tends to zero; this observation could lead them to expect that a maximum volume exists between these two values.

Possible results are given in this table for circles of radius 10 cm. It is unlikely that the pupils' experimental data will be this accurate.

Angle, $\theta°$	Radius of base of cone, cm	Height of cone, cm	Volume of cone, cm³
60	1.7	9.9	29
120	3.3	9.4	110
180	5.0	8.7	227
210	5.8	8.1	289
240	6.7	7.5	347
270	7.5	6.6	389
300	8.3	5.5	402
330	9.2	4.0	352
360	10.0	0	0

The graph shows that the maximum volume occurs when an angle of about 300° is used. For this angle, the volume is 402 cm³.

If Mrs McKinley wants a volume of 250 cm³, the graph shows that two possible angles are available, 191° and 348°. Mrs McKinley should choose 191° as the cone will be easier to make for this value.

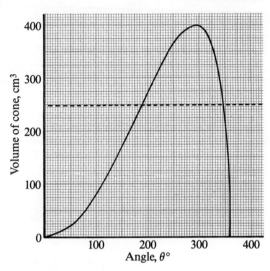

Extensions

A This table gives the volume of the cone (in cm³) for various angles θ° as the radius of the circle takes values from 5 cm to 10 cm. The results are also shown graphically.

	Angle of sector, $\theta°$							
	60	120	180	210	240	270	300	330
Radius, cm	Volume of cone, cm³							
5	4	14	28	36	43	49	50	44
6	6	24	50	63	75	84	87	76
7	10	38	78	99	119	134	138	121
8	15	56	116	148	178	200	206	180
9	21	80	165	211	253	284	293	256
10	29	110	227	289	347	389	402	352

(Note that the maximum of each curve occurs when angle θ is just below 300°.)

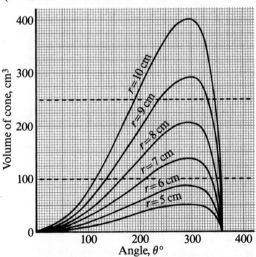

a Yes. Using a circle of radius 9 cm, angles of either 238° or 332°.
b No. The maximum volume obtainable using a 8 cm sector is 207 cm³.
c The graph shows that the radius needed lies between 8 cm and 9 cm. Trial-and-error gives the radius as 8.5 cm to the nearest millimetre.

B Values of angle θ can be read from the graph in **A** above. For $r > 7$, two values of θ are associated with a volume of 100 cm³.

Radius of sector, cm	7	8	9	10
Angles of sector, θ°	211 343	165 353	135 357	114 358

It can also be seen from the graph in **A**, that if 100 cm³ is to be the *maximum* volume, then the radius will be between 6 cm and 7 cm. A better estimate can be found by graphing these results in **B**.

18 · Street lighting

This problem is rather more 'abstract' than many of the earlier ones, and pupils will need to experiment with patterns of circles representing pools of light. In the pupil's book, the second diagram illustrating the problem might help pupils to 'see' where the edges of the road are to be drawn.

The problem

The edges of the road pass through the points of intersection of the circles, so that all points on the road are sufficiently well lit.

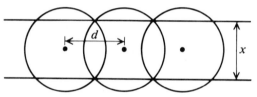

With a radius of 5 cm, the following table gives possible results.

Distance between lamps, d cm	0	2	4	6	8	9	10
Width of road, x cm	10	9.8	9.2	8.0	6.0	4.4	0

4 With lamps 8½ metres apart, the widest possible road is 5.3 metres.

5 a For a road 6 metres wide, the lamps would have to be no more than 8 metres apart.
  b 15 lamps are needed for a road 120 metres long.

6

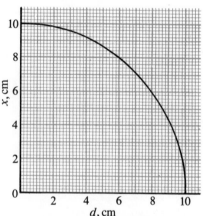

Each lamp can be taken as illuminating a rectangular section of road of area xd.

Using the above graph or table, the following values can be found and then graphed.

d cm	0	2	4	6	8	9	10
xd cm²	0	19.6	36.8	48.0	48.0	39.6	0

The graph suggests that a maximum area of 50 cm² occurs when $d = 7$ cm. From the earlier graph, when $d = 7$ cm, $x = 7$ cm, so to illuminate as great an area as possible, lamps should be placed 7 metres apart in a road 7 metres wide.

Some pupils might be able to find the algebraic relation between x and d using Pythagoras' theorem, viz.

$$x^2 + d^2 = 4r^2$$
$$x^2 + d^2 = 100.$$

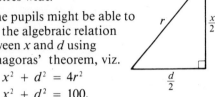
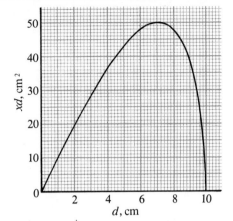

The first graph is thus a quadrant of a circle.
Furthermore, the area $xd = d\sqrt{100 - x^2}$ and the use of a calculator would add further evidence for a maximum value in the region when $d = 7$ cm.

For example, $d = 7$ gives $xd = 49.989999$
$d = 7.1$ gives $xd = 49.998319$
$d = 7.2$ gives $xd = 49.966133.$

A short computer program would generate values quickly for further investigation. (Calculus would *prove* that the maximum value of xd is 50 cm² and occurs when $x = d = 5\sqrt{2}$ cm.)

Extensions

First arrangement
Taking circles of radius 5 cm, the following table gives possible results.

d cm	0	2	4	6	7	8	9	10
x cm	10	11.8	13.2	14.0	14.1	14.0	13.4	10

Note that for the larger values of d, some central areas of the road are not covered by circles. If the lamps are too close together, then a central area is illuminated by all four adjacent lamps. It seems reasonable that the optimum positioning for as wide a road as possible is when four adjacent circles meet at a central point. The graph indicates that this situation occurs when $d = 7$ cm.
(Pupils conversant with Pythagoras' theorem could show that, in this case, $d^2 + d^2 = 4r^2$ so $d = r\sqrt{2} = 7.07$ cm when $r = 5$ cm.)

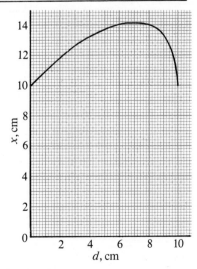

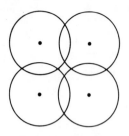
lamps too far apart

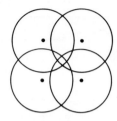
lamps too close

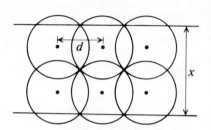
lamps at optimum distance

Comparing the two tables of d and x values, it can be seen that the x values in this paired arrangement can be found by adding the corresponding values of d to the x values in the single arrangement.

Graphically, the curve for the paired arrangement can be found by adding the ordinates for a straight line and a quadrant.

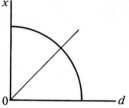

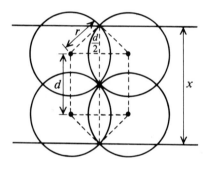

(Abler pupils might be able to find the algebraic relation between d and x, viz.
$$x = d + \sqrt{4r^2 - d^2}$$
$$= d + \sqrt{100 - d^2} \text{ when } r = 5 \text{ cm.}$$

A calculator could now give further evidence of a maximum value of x when $d \simeq 7$ cm.

A short computer program would quickly provide further values.

Calculus would provide a *proof*.)

Second arrangement

Taking circles of radius 5 cm, the following table gives possible results:

d cm	0	2	4	6	7	8	9	10
x cm	10	11.5	12.6	13.2	13.2	12.9	12.2	8.7

Note that for the larger values of d, some central areas of the road are not covered by circles.

The graph indicates that the optimum position for as wide a road as possible occurs when $d \simeq 6.5$ cm.

The road width x is then about 13.2 cm. It is interesting to note that this situation does *not* have adjacent circles passing through the same point as in the first arrangement.

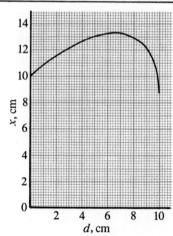

(Pupils able at trigonometry might show that
$$x = \frac{d\sqrt{3}}{2} + \sqrt{4r^2 - d^2}$$
and thus confirm the table of results and explore more closely the position of the maximum value of x using a calculator.

Calculus would show that the maximum value of $5\sqrt{7}$ cm occurs when $d = 5\sqrt{12/7} \simeq 6.55$ cm.)

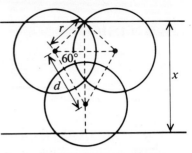

Of these two arrangements, the first illuminates a wider road than the second with lamps which are further apart when placed in the optimum position. The first arrangement is the more economical.

19 · Coils of string

This activity provides a simple context for introducing pupils to the skills of 'curve fitting'. Although the method of 'finding differences' is not a prerequisite some experience of it would be helpful. The use of appropriate computer software is strongly recommended. Two approximations provide two other ways of modelling the problem.

The problem

The following table gives the results which were obtained using 11 coils of an ordinary piece of household string. The experiment could usefully be attempted with strings of different thicknesses.

Number of coils, n	1	2	3	4	5	6	7	8	9	10	11
Length of string used, l cm	2.0	5.4	9.6	14.8	21.0	28.0	36.0	45.1	55.3	66.4	78.7
First difference, $\triangle_1$		3.4	4.2	5.2	6.2	7.0	8.0	9.1	10.2	11.1	12.3
Second difference, $\triangle_2$			0.8	1.0	1.0	0.8	1.0	1.1	1.1	0.9	1.2

The second differences are sufficiently constant to extend the table to predict results for more than eleven coils. Taking $\triangle_2 = 1.0$ gives

10	11	12	13	14
66.4	78.7	92.0		
	12.3	13.3		
1.2	1.0			

and so on, until

10	11	12	13	14
66.4	78.7	92.0	106.3	121.5
	12.3	13.3	14.3	15.3
1.2	1.0	1.0	1.0	

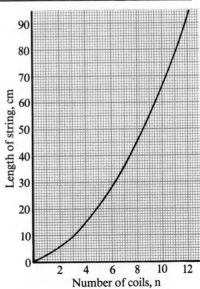

Extensions

A As a further development for pupils who have access to curve-fitting facilities using a computer, the equation relating l to n can be explored. As the second differences are taken as constant, the equation will be of order 2, i.e. $l = an^2 + bn + c$.

B Alternatively, the values of a, b, c can be found algebraically by substituting three sets of results. Taking $n = 0$, 5 and 10 with $l = 0$, 21.0 and 66.4, gives simultaneous equations for a, b, c and hence $l = 0.488n^2 + 1.76n$.
The accuracy of this expression can be checked for (say) $n = 8$ to give $l = 45.3$ compared to the experimental value of $l = 45.1$. The accuracy of the extrapolation process can be checked for (say) $n = 14$ to give $l = 120.3$ compared to the above value of $l = 121.6$.

Two approximations

C For equal areas, $\pi r^2 = lt$ where $r = nt$ so $l = \pi t n^2$.
(Note this expression is also of second degree in n).

The thickness of the string, t can be found using a micrometer or by measuring the overall thickness of several lengths placed together.

The string used for the above result had $t = 0.2$ cm; hence $l = \pi \times 0.2 \times n^2 = 0.63 n^2$.
Note that this expression is very sensitive to variations in t.

n	5	8	10
l	15.8	40.3	63.0

This table shows values of l which underestimate the actual values.

D Knowledge of the sum of an arithmetic progression is needed for this approximation.

With $t = 0.2$ cm, the radii of the first three concentric circles are taken as 0.1, 0.3, 0.5 cm.

So, total length of n coils, $l \simeq$ the sum of the circumferences of n circles

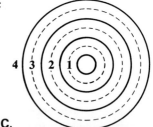

$= 2\pi (r_1 + r_2 + r_3 + \ldots + r_n)$
$= 2\pi (0.1 + 0.3 + 0.5 + \ldots\ldots)$
$= 2\pi \times \dfrac{n}{2} [0.2 + (n - 1) \times 0.2]$
$= 0.63n^2$ which is the same expression as in part **C**.

20 · Stepping along

This is a simple activity to carry out and results are easy to collect. However, it will require a pupil who is a skilled or determined spotter of number patterns to discover the complete pattern. Even so, the teacher should resist 'telling all' to a struggler. The analysis given here is likely not to be the only interpretation.

The problem

1 For pieces which are 6 pips long, the results are:
    steps 1 pip long need 7 pieces before toppling
    steps 2 pips long need 4 pieces before toppling
    steps 3 pips long need 3 pieces before toppling
    steps 4 pips long need 3 pieces before toppling
    steps 5 pips long need 3 pieces before toppling.

2.3 A pattern in the results is complicated. One way forward is to realise that steps of 2 pips using pieces of 6 pips are essentially the same as steps of 1 pip using pieces of 3 pips, i.e. there is just a scale factor involved. It is not, then, the *actual* length of the step which matters, but the *fraction* of the piece used for a step.

An extra column giving this fraction is added to this table of results.

Length of piece, L	Length of step, S	Number of pieces for toppling	Maximum number of pieces for NO toppling, n	Fraction $\frac{S}{L}$
3	1	4	3	$\frac{1}{3}$
	2	3	2	$\frac{2}{3} = 1/1.\dot{6}$
4	1	5	4	$\frac{1}{4}$
	2	3	2	$\frac{1}{2}$
	3	3	2	$\frac{3}{4} = 1/1.\dot{3}$
5	1	6	5	$\frac{1}{5}$
	2	4	3	$\frac{2}{5} = 1/2.5$
	3	3	2	$\frac{3}{5} = 1/1.\dot{6}$
	4	3	2	$\frac{4}{5} = 1/1.25$
6	1	7	6	$\frac{1}{6}$
	2	4	3	$\frac{2}{6} = 1/3$
	3	3	2	$\frac{3}{6} = 1/2$
	4	3	2	$\frac{4}{6} = 1/1.5$
	5	3	2	$\frac{5}{6} = 1/1.2$
8	1	9	8	$\frac{1}{8}$
	2	5	4	$\frac{2}{8} = 1/4$
	3	4	3	$\frac{3}{8} = 1/2.\dot{6}$
	4	3	2	$\frac{4}{8} = 1/2$
	5	3	2	$\frac{5}{8} = 1/1.6$
	6	3	2	$\frac{6}{8} = 1/1.\dot{3}$
	7	3	2	$\frac{7}{8} = 1/1.14$
10	1	11	10	$\frac{1}{10}$
	2	6	5	$\frac{2}{10} = 1/5$
	3	5	4	$\frac{3}{10} = 1/3.\dot{3}$
	4	4	3	$\frac{4}{10} = 1/2.5$
	5	3	2	$\frac{5}{10} = 1/1.2$
	6	3	2	$\frac{6}{10} = 1/1.\dot{6}$
	etc.			

Notice that the fraction $\frac{S}{L}$ has been written with a numerator of 1. A graph of the corresponding denominators, d against the maximum number of pieces for no toppling is interesting. All points are within a narrow band as shown and all points with *integer* coordinates lie on the line $n = d$.

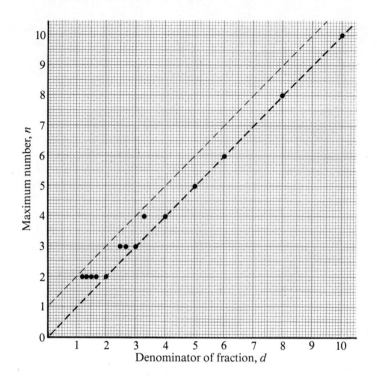

4 One 'rule' for finding the maximum number of pieces for no toppling seems to be:
Write the length of the step as a fraction of the length of the piece and with a numerator of 1. The maximum number of pieces for no toppling is the denominator (if an integer) or the next integer greater than the denominator.

For example, a prediction can be made for steps 3 pips long using pieces 7 pips long. $\frac{3}{7} = 1/2.3$ and 2.3 is not integer; the next greater integer is 3 so 3 steps will balance but 4 steps will topple.

6 Maximum number of pieces for no toppling = 6
so, fraction $\frac{1}{6}$ and step length = $\frac{1}{6} \times 20 = 3\frac{1}{3}$ cm.

There are 12 step lengths across the arch, so distance between walls is $12 \times 3\frac{1}{3} = 40$ cm.

An extension

Provided the midpoint M stays to the left of edge E, then no toppling occurs. (M is the centre of mass of the arrangement).

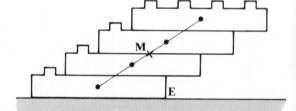

21 · Pins and mirrors

This activity gives rise to number patterns and provides a context for the concept of a discontinuous function. Pupils should be encouraged to note that the symmetry of certain regular polygons has a part to play in the spatial patterns of the pins.

The problem

The tabulated results are as follows:

Angle, $a°$	Number of pins, n
180°	2
90° < a < 180°	3
90°	4
60° < a < 90°	5
60°	6
45° < a < 60°	7
45°	8
36° < a < 45°	9
36°	10
30° < a < 36°	11
30°	12
⋮	⋮

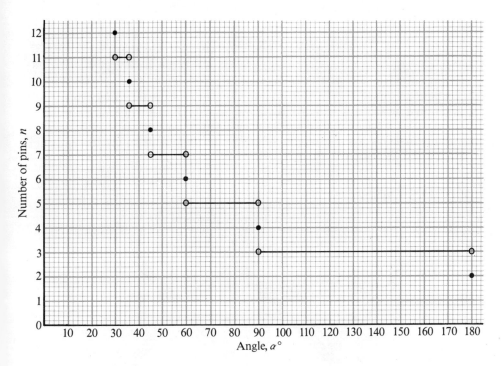

The pattern in the results is:

$n = \dfrac{360}{a}$ for values of a which give *even integer* values of n

and $n =$ the nearest *odd integer* value of $\dfrac{360}{a}$, for all other values of a.

So, $n = 14$ requires $a = \dfrac{360}{14} = 25.7°$ and for $25.7° < a < 30°$, $n = 13$.

Similarly, for smaller angles.

47

5   One customer and four reflections totals 5. Hence any angle between 60° and 90° will suffice. For equally spaced reflections an angle of $\frac{360}{5} = 72°$ is needed.

6   When the mirrors are parallel, $a = 0°$. Theoretically, there is an infinite number of images.

Extensions

A   Except for $n = 2$, the pins stand at the vertices of regular polygons of 4, 6, 8 ... sides.

$n = \frac{360}{\alpha}$ gives $n = 36$ for $\alpha = 10°$.

B   If n is an *odd* integer, then the angle α will be in the range $\frac{360}{n+1} < \alpha < \frac{360}{n-1}$.

Pins which are evenly spaced stand at the vertices of regular polygons of 3, 5, 7 ... sides.

When $\alpha = 11°$, $n = 33$.

When $n = 15$, $22.5° < \alpha < 25.7°$.

22 · Making a pantograph

Prior experience of enlargements (with positive, negative and fractional scale factors) would be a useful prerequisite for this activity. Pupils will need a certain degree of patience and manual dexterity when using a 'home-made' pantograph. Simple commercially-made pantographs are not very expensive to buy, though pupils should try making their own first.

Extensions

A   These dimensions are needed for a length scale factor of 3.

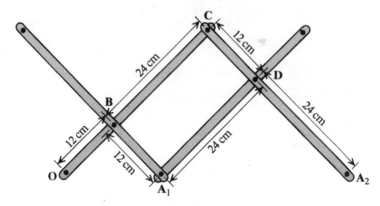

B   In all cases, $OB = BA_1 = CD$ and $BC = A_1D = DA_2$.

The length scale factor, $m = \frac{OC}{OB}$.

When $OC = 36$ cm, the other distances are given by

m	4	5	6	$1\frac{1}{2}$	$2\frac{1}{2}$	$3\frac{1}{2}$
OB	9	7.2	6	24	14.4	10.3 cm
BC	27	28.8	30	12	21.6	25.7 cm

C **a** The images are *reductions* of the object. For example, instead of an enlargement of scale factor 3, the scale factor is $\frac{1}{3}$.

  b The images are now *inverted* when compared to the object. Scale factors will be, for example, -3, or $-\frac{1}{3}$ depending on the positions of the pointer and pencil.

23 · Crank and piston

This simulation of a crank and piston will require a degree of manual dexterity from the pupil. The notion of a function is involved as the distance travelled by the piston depends on the angle rotated by the crank. The activity considers how changes in certain parameters, such as the length of the connecting rod, affect the system.

The problem

Possible results are given in this table:

Angle of rotation of crank, $\theta°$	0	30	60	90	120	150	180	210	240	270	300	330	360
Position of piston, x cm	27.0	26.1	23.7	20.9	18.7	17.4	17.0	17.4	18.7	20.9	23.7	26.1	27.0

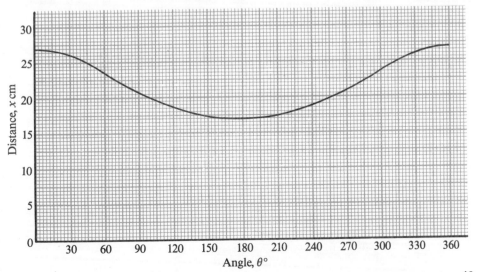

4 a,b When piston P is in its extreme positions, the three moving parts all lie in the same straight line $U_1 U_2 U_3$. In these positions, $x = 17$ cm and $x = 27$ cm.

   c The stroke $= 27 - 17 = 10$ cm

5 The maximum value of angle $U_1 V_2 V_1$ is 24.6°. It occurs when $U_1 V_1$ is perpendicular to the connecting rod R.

Extensions

A Results found by calculation are as follows. It is unlikely that pupils' results from practical activity will be as accurate.

Angle of rotation, $\theta°$		0	30	60	90	120	150	180	210	240	270	300	330	360
Position, x cm	when $U_1 V_1 = 4$ cm	26.0	25.3	23.5	21.3	19.5	18.4	18.0	18.4	19.5	21.3	23.5	25.3	26.0
	when $U_1 V_1 = 6$ cm	28.0	26.8	23.8	20.4	17.8	16.4	16.0	16.4	17.8	20.4	23.8	26.8	28.0
	when $U_1 V_1 = 8$ cm	30.0	28.2	23.8	18.9	15.8	14.4	14.0	14.4	15.8	18.9	23.8	28.2	30.0
	when $U_1 V_1 = 10$ cm	32.0	29.6	23.3	16.6	13.3	12.2	12.0	12.2	13.3	16.6	23.3	29.6	32.0

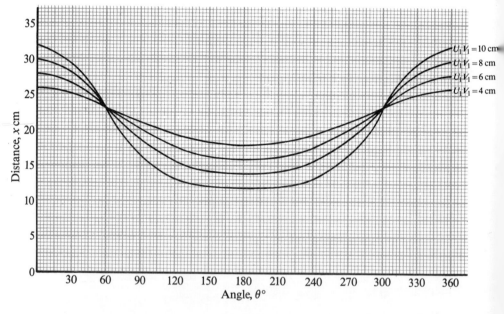

The larger is the radius of the crank, the larger is the stroke of the piston.

Radius of crank $U_1 V_1$, cm	Length of stroke, cm
4	$26 - 18 = 8$
5	$27 - 17 = 10$
6	$28 - 16 = 12$
8	$30 - 14 = 16$
10	$32 - 12 = 20$

From which it can be deduced:
 Length of stroke $= 2 \times$ radius of crank.

B Results from the practical activity will not be as accurate as the following calculated results.

Angle of rotation, $\theta°$		0	30	60	90	120	150	180	210	240	270	300	330	360
Position, x cm	when $V_1V_2 = 10$ cm	25.0	24.0	21.5	18.7	16.5	15.4	15.0	15.4	16.5	18.7	21.5	24.0	25.0
	when $V_1V_2 = 12$ cm	27.0	26.1	23.7	20.9	18.7	17.4	17.0	17.4	18.7	20.9	23.7	26.1	27.0
	when $V_1V_2 = 14$ cm	29.0	28.1	25.8	23.1	20.8	19.4	19.0	19.4	20.8	23.1	25.8	28.1	29.0
	when $V_1V_2 = 16$ cm	31.0	30.1	27.9	25.2	22.9	21.5	21.0	21.5	22.9	25.2	27.9	30.1	31.0

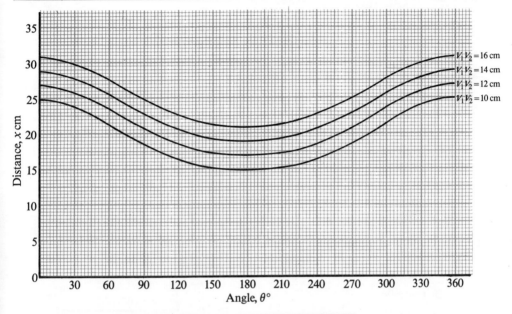

Length of connecting rod V_1V_2, cm	Length of stroke, cm
10	25 − 15 = 10
12	27 − 17 = 10
14	29 − 19 = 10
16	31 − 21 = 10

The length of the connecting rod has no effect on the length of the stroke of the piston.

C

	Radius of crank U_1V_1, cm	Length of connecting rod V_1V_2, cm
a	$\frac{12}{2} = 6$	6 + 8 = 14
b	$\frac{10}{2} = 5$	13.7
c	$\frac{10}{2} = 5$	2 × 5 = 10

In **c**, the minimum length of V_1V_2 is $2 \times U_1V_1$ because a shorter connecting rod would have the piston P colliding with the crank wheel C.

D With the radius of the crank wheel, r and the length of the connecting rod, l and the length of the piston, p, the distance x is given
$$p + r\cos\theta + \sqrt{l^2 - r^2\sin^2\theta}.$$

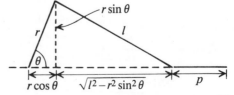

24 · Manoeuvring around corners

This activity is made 2-dimensional as the tube is at all times in contact with the floor. The length of the longest possible tube is seen as a function of the width of the corridor and a simple algebraic relationship can be found.

The problem

3 Possible results are given in this table.

Width of corridor, m	5	6	7	8	9	10
Length of longest tube, m	14.1	17.0	19.8	22.6	25.5	28.3

4 Gradient of straight line = 2.83.
Relationship between length of longest tube, l and width of corridor, w is $l = 2.83 \times w$.
(An extra row, $\frac{l}{w}$ added to the above table is particularly convincing also.)

5 Using either the graph or the equation $l = 2.83 \times w$, the longest tube has a length of
   a 18.4 metres
   b 11.3 metres.

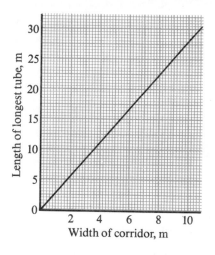

Extensions

A

Angle, $a°$	90	80	70	60	50	40	30	20
Length of longest possible tube, m	14.1	15.6	17.4	20.0	23.7	29.2	38.6	57.6

Pupils' results will be acceptable even though they may be much less accurate than those given here.

As angle a gets smaller, longer tubes can be manoeuvred around the corner. Eventually, when $a = 0°$, there is no corner and the tube can be infinitely long.

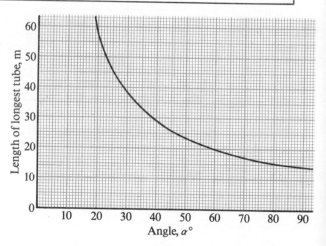

If a pupil is unsure when the longest tube is *half-way* round, the question might be asked "Where will the midpoint of the tube be when half-way round?" or even "Will the situation be symmetrical when it is half-way round?"

B

Angle of corner, $a°$	90	80	70	60	50	40	30	20
Angle between tube and wall when half-way round	45	40	35	30	25	20	15	10

The angle between tube and wall is half the angle of the corner when half-way round. (At this point the tube is in a symmetrical position with respect to the wall.)

Trigonometry gives $DZ = \dfrac{5}{\sin\frac{a}{2}}$

so length of tube $YZ = \dfrac{10}{\sin\frac{a}{2}}$.

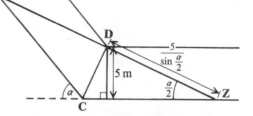

25 · Wrapping a parcel

This activity requires an ability to 'spot the number pattern' in the results, but the pattern can be seen to arise as a consequence of the folding activity when the wrapping paper is brought in contact with the cuboid. The activity lends itself to introducing, in context, a generalisation for the area of paper in algebraic terms.

The problem

Most commercial packets are now designed to metric measurements but the dimensions are not always of a size where number patterns are easy to spot. The teacher might provide a selection of cuboids of commercial manufacture together with a few home-made ones of more straightforward dimensions, e.g. 10 cm × 6 cm × 5 cm or 15 cm × 12 cm × 10 cm.

Possible results are as follows and might include the names of the article.

Edges A and B folded first:

Object	Dimension of cuboid			Size of smallest wrapping paper		
	length, l cm	breadth, b cm	height, h cm	length, L cm	breadth, B cm	area, A cm²
Cereal packet	25	19	5	30	48	1440
Packet of tea bags	19	13	7	26	40	1040
Packet of tea	13	6	5	18	22	396
Paperback book	18	11	3	21	28	588
Other cuboids {	10	6	5	15	22	330
	15	12	10	25	44	1100

Edges X and Y folded first:

Object	Dimension of cuboid			Size of smallest wrapping paper		
	length, l cm	breadth, b cm	height, h cm	length, L cm	breadth, B cm	area, A cm^2
Cereal packet	25	19	5	60	24	1440
Packet of tea bags	19	13	7	52	20	1040
Packet of tea	13	6	5	36	11	396
Paperback book	18	11	3	42	14	588
Other cuboids	10	6	5	30	11	330
	15	12	10	50	22	1100

When edges A and B are folded first,
$L = l + h$
$B = 2(b + h)$.

When edges Y and Z are folded first,
$L = 2(l + h)$
$B = b + h$.

The area of the smaller size of wrapping paper is the same in both cases.

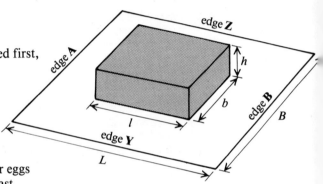

The box containing the Easter eggs requires wrapping paper at least 23 cm × 36 cm or 18 cm × 46 cm, in both cases having an area of 828 cm^2.

The birthday present requires wrapping paper at least 46 cm × 28 cm or 92 cm × 14 cm, in both cases having an area of 1288 cm^2.

Note: In all the above, the 'length' of a cuboid has been taken as the longest of its three dimensions, the 'breadth' as the second longest dimension, and the 'height' as the shortest dimension. If the words 'length', 'breadth' and 'height' are allowed to refer to any of the three dimensions, then six possibilities can occur. Pupils might be asked to consider these possibilities; for example, for the Easter egg box above:

l	b	h	$L = l + h$	$B = 2(b + h)$	A, cm^2
15	10	8	23	36	828
15	8	10	25	36	900
10	15	8	18	46	828
10	8	15	25	46	1150
8	15	10	18	50	900
8	10	15	23	50	1150

These results prompt the question "How can we be sure when wrapping a cuboid that our result will be *the* smallest possible?"

Extensions

A When edges A and B are folded first, $L = 2(l + h) = 30$
$$B = b + h = 20.$$

Substituting values of h, gives these results for possible cuboids:

Height, h cm	2	4	6	8	10	12	14
Length, l cm	13	11	9	7	5	3	1
Breadth, b cm	18	16	14	12	10	8	6
Volume, V cm³	468	704	756	672	500	288	84

When edges Y and Z are folded first, $L = l + h = 30$
$$B = 2(b + h) = 20.$$

Substituting values of h, gives these results for possible cuboids:

Height, h cm	2	4	5	6	7	8
Length, l cm	28	26	25	24	23	22
Breadth, b cm	8	6	5	4	3	2
Volume, V cm³	448	624	625	576	483	352

B The maximum volume occurs when the cuboid's dimensions are approximately 14 cm × 9 cm × 6 cm, in which case the 9 cm dimension is placed parallel to the 30 cm edge of the wrapping paper and the 20 cm edges of the paper are folded first.

A more accurate value of the maximum volume can be found using a calculator, e.g.

h	l	b	V
5.0 cm	10.0 cm	15.0 cm	750 cm³
5.5 cm	9.5 cm	14.5 cm	757.625 cm³
5.7 cm	9.3 cm	14.3 cm	758.043 cm³
5.8 cm	9.2 cm	14.2 cm	757.712 cm³

from which it seems that a maximum volume occurs when $5.5 \text{ cm} < h < 5.8 \text{ cm}$. Further calculation will reduce this range.
(Calculus *proves* that a maximum volume of 758.1 cm³ occurs when $h = 5.66$ cm, to 2 decimal places).

C A sheet of A4 paper is 210 mm × 297 mm.
When edges A and B are folded first, $2(l + h) = 297$
$$b + h = 210.$$

Substituting values of h gives these results for possible cuboids:

Height, h mm	20	30	40	50	60	70	80
Length, l mm	128.5	118.5	108.5	98.5	88.5	78.5	68.5
Breadth, b mm	190	180	170	160	150	140	130
Volume, V mm³	488 300	639 900	737 800	788 000	796 500	769 300	712 400

A maximum volume appears to exist in the range $50 \text{ mm} < h < 70 \text{ mm}$. Further exploration by calculator gives a volume of 797 971.5 mm³ when $h = 57$ mm.
A computer program could be used to speed up the calculations.

When edges X and Y are folded first, $l + h = 297$
$$2(b + h) = 210$$

Substituting values of h as before gives a maximum volume of approximately 680 000 mm³ when $h = 50$ mm. This maximum is not as great as the previous one. Thus, the greatest volume of a cuboid which can be wrapped in a sheet of A4 paper is 798 cm³ when the dimensions of the cuboid are 57 mm × 91.5 mm × 153 mm.

26 · Free gifts with breakfast cereal

A simple simulation is undertaken using dice and gives a context for preliminary ideas of probability, although no prior knowledge or understanding of probability is needed, and the word 'probability' need not be used in the activity if the teacher so wishes. Pupils might also be shown how to use random number tables instead of dice in order to speed up the process of obtaining results. Pupils can then be challenged to design their own simulations for the three further problems.

Introduction

The manufacturer might be tempted to make fewer of one of the tokens so that collectors have to buy more 'Snapwheat' to get a full set of tokens. This ploy would not be 'fair'. If several people are collecting tokens and all of them have difficulty collecting one particular token, their suspicions might be aroused.

The six faces of an ordinary dice can represent the six different tokens. Rolling the dice then represents buying one packet of 'Snapwheat'. The assumption is implied that the manufacturer is 'fair'.

Simulation

These results were obtained for 12 trials.

Trial	Scores on dice (i.e. tokens collected)	Number of throws needed (i.e. packets bought)
1	132264412635	12
2	351621562611631525355235516654	30
3	523255461	9
4	61331361554556636563613642	26
5	5656623533552113263535131562552632535124	40
6	61611432612311145	17
7	16355561552364	14
8	6353215322514	13
9	6266512334	10
10	35462421	8
11	16343352	8
12	53545532655353445565446341	26

The average number of throws in these twelve trials is 213/12 = 17.8 but, as the number of throws varies from 8 to 40, considerably more results will be needed before the average can be taken as an accurate value of the expected number of packets needing to be bought. (It can be shown theoretically that the expected number of packets for a full set of tokens is 14.7 in which case you can expect to spend 14.7 × 50p = £7·35 before getting a free cereal bowl. As 60 ÷ 14.7 ≃ 4.1, the manufacturer would need to increase the price of each packet by 4 pence for the scheme *almost* to pay for itself, though this calculation assumes that *all* customers are saving *all* their tokens for free bowls.)

The scheme is not particularly attractive to customers as 15 packets on average are needed for a free bowl which requires a good deal of perseverance on the customer's part – many might not bother or give up. The scheme is only attractive to the manufacturer if it encourages customers to buy more 'Snapwheat' — if the bowls are attractive, this might be the case until customers realise how many packets they might have to buy.

Extensions

A The simulation could be altered, for example, *either* by using an eleven-sided spinner with B to F having two sections each and A only one, *or* by using the dice as before, except that it requires *two* throws of (say) a 6 before token A is said to have been collected. More packets will need to be bought, on average, and an experiment can determine an approximate value of the expected number.

B Fewer packets would, on average, be needed for the second bowl. An experiment would determine an approximate value of the expected number of packets.

27 · Radioactive decay

This simulation, in addition to giving another context for introducing a simulation and the notion of probability, provides a practical way of gaining an understanding of how radioactivity 'works' and what half-life means.

Simulation

Possible results, starting with 100 drawing pins, could be:

	After these units of time												
	0	1	2	3	4	5	6	7	8	9	10	11	12
Number of atoms still radioactive	100	57	37	18	9	5	3	2	2	1	1	1	0
Number of atoms decayed	0	43	63	82	91	95	97	98	98	99	99	99	100

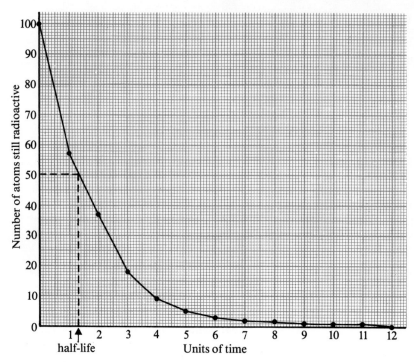

In the above trial, all atoms had decayed after 12 units of time and half of them after 1.3 units of time (the *half-life*).

Repeating the trial several times and averaging the results will produce a smoother graph and a more accurate estimate of the half-life.

Problems

6   **a**   25 grams   **b**   0.5 grams

7   about 0.31 kg

8   nearly 50 thousand years (48 780 years)

9   4860 years

10   In every 50 years, half of the radioactive atoms will decay. Using the constant function on a calculator to divide 10^{22} by 2 over and over again, the following values can be found:

Time, years	0	500	1000	1500	2000	2500	3000	3500
Number of atoms still radioactive	10^{22}	9.8×10^{18}	9.5×10^{15}	9.3×10^{12}	9.1×10^{9}	8.9×10^{6}	8700	8

It will take over 3500 years for all 10 grams to decay.

Extensions

A   **a**   (i)   For a quickly decaying substance, remove rice (or counters) which fall on *unshaded* squares.
               The half life is about 0.5 units of time.

       (ii)   For a slowly decaying substance, remove rice (or counters) which fall on *shaded* squares.
               The half-life is about 2.4 units of time.

   b   To simulate even slower decay, fewer shaded squares are needed.

c To simulate Iodine-131, only $\frac{1}{12} \times 36 = 3$ squares need to be shaded. Rice falling on these 3 squares represent atoms which are no longer radioactive.

This simulation should be repeated several times for an average value to be found. The half-life of Iodine-131 is 8 days.

B Each digit from 0 to 9 represents an atom. When the digit is 0 the atom decays; when the digit is 1 to 9 the atom stays radioactive.

The simulation is started with a given number of atoms (say 12); the larger the number, the more accurate the result. Choose the first 12 digits on the first row of the random number table — this represents a time of 1 hour.

    14   05   84   30   11   24

The two 0s indicate that 2 atoms have decayed in this hour. Now choose the next 10 random numbers.

    98   63   45   28   61

No atoms have decayed in this hour. Now choose the next 10 numbers.

    39   06   56   28   60

Two 0s indicate that 2 atoms have decayed in this hour. Now choose a further 8 numbers, and continue the process until 6 atoms are left. As 6 is half of the original 12, the time passed is an estimate of the *half-life*.

Repeat many times, starting at different places in the table and moving in different directions through the table. Find the average of the results.

The half-life of Palladium-234 is 6.6 hours.

28 · In a nuclear reactor

This simulation can be used to see how results are affected by changes in the problem's parameters; namely, the 'life' of a neutron (simulated by one throw of the dice for each second of life) and the thickness of the reactor's shielding (simulated by the size of the triangular tessellation). A speedier way of obtaining results is to use random number tables, ignoring the digits 0, 7, 8 and 9.

Simulation

Once a neutron has escaped from the shielding, it does not re-enter. Fewer than half the neutrons are held in the shielding after 5 seconds; this situation is most certainly not acceptable.

Extensions

A If too many neutrons are escaping, an extra layer of shielding is required as shown here. Only about $\frac{1}{5}$ of the neutrons now escape. Even this proportion might be considered too high, in which case yet another layer of shielding could be added.

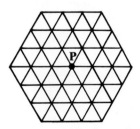

B If a neutron has less initial energy, then it will have less time to make its escape. Only 4 rolls of the dice would simulate a time of 4 seconds before it had so little energy that escape was impossible.

Six rolls of the die would simulate a *more* energetic neutron.

C In tracking all the possible paths of the neutrons, it is best to start with neutrons of little energy.

Neutrons which last 1 second arrive in one of six positions, all of them identical.

Neutrons which last 2 seconds arrive in the positions shown on the right. None escape.

Neutrons which last 3 seconds arrive in positions indicated by a 3 on the following diagrams.

The popularity of these positions after 3 seconds is shown on this diagram.

Of these 36 positions, 7 are outside the shielding. We can thus expect $\frac{7}{36} \simeq 0.2$ of neutrons to escape.

Neutrons which last 4 seconds arrive in positions indicated by a 4 on the following diagrams. (Possibilities not indicated here are reflections or rotations of those shown.)

There are 6 × 36 = 216 different routes for 4 seconds of which 7 × 6 = 42 have already led to an escape after 3 seconds. Using the diagram showing the popularity of positions after 3 seconds, there a further
(2 × 3) + (2 × 2) + (2 × 3) + (1 × 2) + (2 × 2) + (2 × 3) + (1 × 2) = 30 other escape routes. We can thus expect $\frac{42 + 30}{216} = \frac{1}{3}$ of neutrons to escape after 4 seconds.

In summary,

Life of neutron	1	2	3	4
Fraction escaping	0	0	$\frac{1}{5}$	$\frac{1}{3}$

A life of 5 seconds can be investigated in a similar way, though the possible routes are more complicated to list.

29 · Queuing at the corner shop

This activity is the first and simpler of two queuing simulations. After using dice, spinners and/or coins to obtain results, some pupils may appreciate the use of random number tables; e.g. digits 1, 2, 3 can simulate Mrs Garforth finishing serving a customer, digits 4 to 9 *not* finishing and digit 0 is ignored. A computer program could provide a third way of carrying out the simulation.

Simulation

1. With a coin, *heads* can represent one customer arriving and *tails* no customer arriving, in any given minute.
   With a dice or spinner, *even* scores can represent one customer arriving and *odd* scores none arriving.

2. In any given minute, the probability that Mrs Garforth finishes serving a customer is $\frac{1}{3}$. On a dice or spinner, scores of 1 and 2 can represent finishing serving a customer, other scores 4 to 6 that she does not finish serving in that minute. (A coin is little use in representing an event which has a probability of $\frac{1}{3}$.)

3. Possible results are:

During the	Number in queue at start of minute	Result of first throw	Does anyone join the queue? yes/no	Result of second throw	Does anyone leave the queue? yes/no	Number in queue at end of minute
1st	0	4	yes	5	no	1
2nd	1	4	yes	4	no	2
3rd	2	1	no	6	no	2
4th	2	5	no	4	no	2
5th	2	1	no	1	yes	1
6th	1	5	no	1	yes	0
7th	0	1	no	4	no	0
8th	0	4	yes	2	yes	0
9th	0	2	yes	5	no	1
10th	1	2	yes	6	no	2
11th	2	6	yes	6	no	3
12th	3	8	yes	2	yes	3
13th	3	2	yes	2	yes	3
14th	3	5	no	4	no	3
15th	3	4	yes	6	no	4
16th	4	4	yes	6	no	5
17th	5	4	yes	1	yes	5
18th	5	3	no	4	no	5
19th	5	5	no	3	no	5
20th	5	3	no	2	yes	4
21st	4	1	no	2	yes	3
22nd	3	6	yes	6	no	4
23rd	4	5	no	6	no	4
24th	4	2	yes	4	no	5
25th minute	5	4	yes	3	no	6

4. Although the length of the queue fluctuates, there is a gradual build-up of customers waiting to be served.

   If the queue gets too long, people who arrive will not be prepared to wait and will leave straight away — the simulation does not take account of this happening.

   Mrs Garforth needs to be able to call on extra help every now and then.

Extensions

A With fewer than 4 customers (as before):

    first throw
    even score = customer arriving
    odd score = no new customer

    second throw
    1 or 2 = finishes serving a customer
    3, 4, 5 or 6 = continues serving same customer.

With 4 or more customers:

    first throw
    as before

    second throw
    1, 2, 3 or 4 = finishes serving a customer
    5 or 6 = continues serving same customers.

With the son also serving, the probability of finishing serving a customer in any given minute rises to $\frac{2}{3}$.

During the	Number in queue at start of minute	Result of first throw	Does anyone join the queue? yes/no	Result of second throw	Does anyone leave the queue? yes/no	Number in queue at end of minute
1st	0	1	no	4	no	0
2nd	0	2	yes	4	no	1
3rd	1	3	no	1	yes	0
4th	0	1	no	2	(no queue)	0
5th	0	4	yes	6	no	1
6th	1	3	no	4	no	1
7th	1	5	no	2	yes	0
8th	0	6	yes	1	yes	0
9th	0	4	yes	6	no	1
10th	1	5	no	6	no	1
11th	1	2	yes	6	no	2
12th	2	1	no	1	yes	1
13th	1	6	yes	3	no	2
14th	2	5	no	4	no	2
15th	2	6	yes	4	no	3
16th	3	2	yes	4	no	4
17th	4 (A)	2	yes	3	yes	4
18th	4	4	yes	3	yes	4
19th	4	1	no	6	no	4
20th	4	6	yes	6	no	5
21st	5	1	no	3	yes	4
22nd	4	5	no	2	yes	3 (B)
23rd	3	4	yes	5	no	4
24th	4 (A)	4	yes	1	yes	4
25th minute	4	5	no	3	yes	3 (B)

At the positions marked (*A*), Mrs Garforth's son lends a hand; at positions marked (*B*), he leaves. His presence in this simulation seems to stabilise the length of the queue, but the simulation needs to go on longer to see what long term effect he has.

A longer simulation is needed to see how much Mrs Garforth's son is used before it can be said whether it would be worthwhile having a full-time assistant.

A computer program which performs this simulation would be helpful.

B Mr George's garage

1, 2 or 3 cars being equally likely to join the queue can be simulated by rolling a dice:

    score 1 or 4 = 1 car joins queue
    score 2 or 5 = 2 cars join queue
    score 3 or 6 = 3 cars join queue

No car or just one car joining the queue can be simulated by rolling a dice:

    even score = no car joins queue
    odd score = 1 car joins queue

The following table gives possible results. Scores in brackets indicate that 4 or more cars are queuing and that the meaning attached to the value of the scores changes. Note also that, in calculating the number of cars queuing at the end of the minute, Mr George will have served one customer during the minute, so the total is reduced by 1. It is assumed that there is no queue at 5 p.m.

Time of day, minutes past 5 p.m.	0	1	2	3	4	5	6	7	8	9	10	11	12	13	14	15	16	17	18	19	20	21	22	23	24	25	26	27	28	29	30
Cars in queue at start of minute	0	0	0	1	1	3	3	4	3	5	5	4	4	3	5	5	5	4	4	3	4	3	3	3	5	4	4	4	3	3	5
Score on dice	1	4	5	4	3	1	2	(4)	6	(3)	(4)	(5)	(2)	6	(1)	(3)	(6)	(5)	(6)	2	(6)	1	1	6	(2)	(5)	(3)	(4)	4	3	(2)
Number joining queue	1	1	2	1	3	1	2	0	3	1	0	1	0	3	1	1	0	1	0	2	0	1	1	3	0	1	1	0	1	3	0
Cars in queue at end of minute	0	0	1	1	3	3	4	3	5	5	4	4	3	5	5	5	4	4	3	4	3	3	3	5	4	4	4	3	3	5	4

63

In this simulation, the queue quickly builds up to 4 cars and thereafter there are always 3, 4 or 5 cars in the queue. Mr George is kept busy but he is coping. A longer simulation is needed to find out whether the queue increases in length and how Mr George fares if it does so, but by then the 'rush hour' might be over.

To speed up the simulation, random number tables could be used instead of a dice, in which case numbers other than 1 to 6 are ignored completely.

30 · Queuing at the supermarket

This final and more complicated simulation should prove an interesting challenge for pupils who have shown themselves to be confident with simpler simulations.

Introduction

The main features of the simulation are the number of customers arriving at the tills, the number of assistants at the tills and the length of time taken to serve a customer.

Ideally, each customer arrives at a till just as the previous customer is leaving. With too few tills, queues form; with too many tills, the assistants are left waiting for customers.

Simulation

The average number of customers arriving in each 2-minute interval = 4.5.
The average time required to serve a customer = 150 seconds.
So, the serving time needed at the tills in each 2-minute interval
= 4.5 × 150 = 675 seconds.
Hence, the number of tills required = 675 ÷ 120 = 6 to the nearest integer.

If it is felt that serving times of less than (say) 10 seconds are unrealistic, then results outside the range of 10 to 300 can be ignored and the above arithmetic altered accordingly.

The possible number of customers arriving at the tills can be altered in the simulation *either* by changing the upper limit on the accepted range of random number *or* by changing the scores on the dice.

The extensions will require long pieces of graph paper.

Extension **B** is lengthy and pupils might collaborate in drawing their comparisons.